PEMBROKESHIRE 2000
Land and People

Brian John

Greencroft Books

Computer typesetting and design
by the author
Printing by Gwasg Gomer,
Llandysul

First Published 1999
ISBN 0 905559 78 9

Twelve of the photographs in this
book, namely those on the front
cover, title page, and pages
5,30,31,34,64,66,75,102,105, and111,
were taken by Martin John.
All others are by the author.

**This book is dedicated to Callum,
who will help to shape the new
Millennium**

**Greencroft Books, Trefelin,
Cilgwyn, Newport,
Pembrokeshire SA42 0QN
Tel: 01239-820470**

Lists of Illustrations

SECTION THREE. RECENT CHANGES IN THE LANDSCAPE

Preface

This book is a celebration of the county of Pembrokeshire at the beginning of a new Millennium. It is largely a photographic portrait of scenic beauty. But not everything in Pembrokeshire is beautiful and washed with pastel shades, and in the pages that follow you will find photographs of many features that are functional and even unattractive to the eye. But they contribute to the personality of Pembrokeshire today, and so I have chosen to include them. The format of the book follows closely that of "The Pembrokeshire Landscape", prepared by photographer Robert Evans and

Carn Edward
(Martin John)

myself for Five Arches Press in 1973. It was well received, but went rapidly out of print and was never reprinted. In preparing this new volume, I have had two objectives in mind -- namely to paint a vivid and multi-dimensional picture of the old and new county, and to provide a reliable and up-to-date commentary in the text which accompanies the photographs. The book is subtitled "Land and People"; the reader will find that while the photographs portray the county's landscape, the text is concerned above all else with the people who have, at various stages of our history, built and inhabited the buildings, worked the land, and generally left their mark on almost everything.

References in the captions are numbered, and are listed at the end of the book. Each of the plates is numbered and located with the help of a grid reference. The reader is recommended to refer constantly to O.S. 1:50,000 Landranger maps 145, 157 and 158, and 1:25,000 Outdoor Leisure Maps 35 and 36. These maps are not only useful for finding your way about, but they provide a huge amount of detail about the local history revealed in the landscape.

Introduction

The Pembrokeshire landscape is known and loved by many thousands of residents and visitors. In particular, they love the magnificent and varied coastline, recognised by the government through the creation of the Pembrokeshire Coast National Park. In both the coastal and inland sections of the Park there are wide expanses of remote and unspoilt cliff scenery and countryside, with small pockets of settlement.

The environment in which we live has two main constituents: the natural inheritance of bedrock, landforms, climate and plant and animal life, and the cultural inheritance derived from many generations of human activity. The interactions between these two components are many and complex; man's occupation of territory is influenced in innumerable ways by the dictates of natural phenomena, but he in turn has modified the natural environment to suit himself. Often these deliberate modifications have worked to man's advantage, but other changes have been detrimental.

The book is divided into three parts. Section One is concerned with the features of the natural landscape —its plateau surfaces, its streams, its coastline, its rock outcrops. In Section Two we are concerned with man-made features of some antiquity; these are considered in decreasing order of age from the megalithic monuments of the Stone Age through a number of historical phases. Section Three of the book is concerned with "Pembrokeshire today," and shows some of the manifestations of the economic and other changes which have taken place in the last decades of the twentieth century.

At the outset, it is useful to point out some of the more important themes in the history and geography of Pembrokeshire.

1. The rocks which form the foundations of Pembrokeshire range from the immensely old Precambrian rocks of the St. David's area to the recent deposits of the Ice Age and the blown sands and estuarine muds which have accumulated during the past 10,000 years. Overall, Pembrokeshire belongs to the Palaeozoic province of Great Britain, with hardly any solid rocks less than 200 million years old. Nevertheless, most of the physical features which we see today

are relatively youthful, as we shall see in the first section of the book.

2. The natural diversity of the Pembrokeshire landscape is striking, and this gives rise to much of its beauty. On the coast there are long spectacular cliffed stretches with caves, arches, narrow peninsulas and high headlands, and occasional wide sandy bays or narrow secluded tidal inlets. Inland there are the bleak rolling moorlands of the Preseli uplands and the rocky hills of Pen Caer. And further south there is the peaceful Daugleddau estuary, whose character changes with the ebb and flow of every tide. But many areas off the beaten tourist track are no less attractive; in particular, the warm well-wooded landscape of central Pembrokeshire, the bright expanse of the Milford Haven waterway, and the deep gashes of Treffgarne Gorge, Nant-y-bugail and Esgyrn Bottom.

3. Cultural diversity is added by the basic division of the county into two regions of more or less equal size, divided by an invisible boundary called the Landsker. The southern region is traditionally known as the Englishry, or as "Little England beyond Wales." Here the landscape is gentle, intensively farmed and occasionally well-wooded.

Farms look prosperous, and there are larger villages and towns than in the north. Place-names are predominantly Anglo-Saxon, and stone castles and "English" churches with tall, battlemented towers are noticeable. In the north the landscape of the Welshry is wilder and in many respects less modified by the hand of man. Here there are small dispersed farmsteads and isolated hamlets. There are no large towns. Place-names are generally Welsh, and the Welsh language is still widely spoken. There are only a few stone castles, and churches are for the most part small and simple with open bellcotes. Without doubt, in north Pembrokeshire we are in a part of Celtic Wales.

4. When we look at the towns of Pembrokeshire, we notice a contrast between the old market towns and the "new towns" of the nineteenth century. The older towns of Haverfordwest, Pembroke and Tenby still retain traces of their medieval functions as military bases for the Normans and as service centres for the Englishry. To a more limited extent, the smaller towns of St. David's, Fishguard, Narberth and Newport also developed as market centres. The Haven towns of Milford, Neyland and Pembroke Dock owe most of

their growth to the nineteenth century, when the potential of the deep-water harbour was at last realised. The grid-iron street-patterns, the clear signs of urban planning, and the more recent buildings of these towns make them quite distinct from their older neighbours. They are also associated with industrial and port activities on the Haven.

5. The Pembrokeshire Coalfield has played an important part in the geography of the county. At least since the fourteenth century, high quality anthracite has been won from the Coal Measures, which stretches from St. Bride's Bay to the Daugleddau and thence to Saundersfoot Bay. By 1900 there were local colliery landscapes in several districts, but by 1947 the county's "industrial revolution" was ended. Now the hand of time has largely obscured the traces of coal mining, although the extraction of slate, limestone and igneous rock has left a number of larger scars on the landscape. The extractive industries were never developed on a sufficient scale to destroy the rural character of the county.

6. Pembrokeshire still has a large farming community, and until recently most of the people of the county depended for their livelihood upon

activities directly or indirectly connected with agriculture. For many centuries the county was renowned for the quality of its crops, and arable farming is still of importance particularly in the Englishry. The county is of course well known for its early potatoes. These are generally grown in a narrow coastal strip, where the equable climate often makes it possible for local "earlies" to reach the English market before the end of May. But the keeping of livestock is everywhere important, with dairying, stock rearing for meat, and sheep farming all widespread. Currently there is a real crisis in the farming industry, with milk and meat over-production, reduced farm subsidies from Europe, and the BSE crisis all responsible to some degree.

7. Tourism is now Pembrokeshire's major industry. Well over a million visitors stay in the coastal resorts every year, and there is now a peak holiday accommodation of over 90,000 beds. Most "family" groups prefer the twin resorts of Tenby and Saundersfoot, but there are numerous other smaller holiday centres around the coast. Of these, Broad Haven, St. David's, Freshwater East and Newport have seen considerable growth, and there is now a demand for prime self-catering accommodation throughout the National Park. The Pembrokeshire

regattas have added essential colour to the summer scene for well over forty years. There is an inexorable rise in the popularity of walking on the Coast Path and on the county's wonderful network of inland paths, and activity holidays of various types are attractive to the younger generation in particular. Twenty years ago there were hardly any major "all weather" attractions in Pembrokeshire; now there are many, including Oakwood and Folly Farm in the centre of the county.

8. Probably the most important feature of present-day Pembrokeshire is the contrast between the industrialized shores of Milford Haven and the rural calm of the rest of the county. Real industrialisation came to Pembrokeshire after a long period of underdevelopment, and in the period 1955 - 1975 four oil refineries and another oil terminal and tank farm were built on the Haven. Vast new oil jetties were thrust into the waterway, and iron and concrete structures pushed skywards. In addition, a new power-station was built at Pennar near Pembroke Dock. A new reservoir was built at Llysyfran to provide industrial water, and the Cleddau Bridge was built as a strategic link between the north and south industrial complexes. In spite of the undoubted economic advantages brought to the county by these developments, the huge numbers of jobs promised by the oil companies never materialised. Concern was felt by many people from the outset because much of the industrial area was sited within the National Park, and there was some unease over pollution risks. The county's "Oil Age" is now in decline. There are only two refineries left on stream. Pembroke Power Station is closed, and due for demolition. And in a last vengeful act, cruel fate sent the supertanker "Sea Empress" aground at the mouth of Milford Haven in February 1996, spilling 72,000 tonnes of crude oil into the precious coastal waters of Pembrokeshire.......

Several of the above points have been concerned with the contrasts or cultural differences which can be recognized within Pembrokeshire. One should not, however, forget that there is a real sense of unity in the old county. From a historical point of view, everyone shares a common heritage. The phases which have influenced the Pembrokeshire countryside have left their mark on all the regions of the county to a greater or lesser extent. The natural environments of north and south have more in common than one is often led to believe, and there is a danger of over-emphasising the differences which may exist between life in the Welshry and life in the Englishry, especially since there is something of a Welsh-language resurgence under way.

These then are some of the themes which are illustrated and described in more detail in the pages which follow. I have tried to select meaningful features of the Pembrokeshire landscape, but I have deliberately concentrated upon many features which are not particularly prominent or well-known in the local scene. There is a very good reason for this. While it may be true that much of what we see in the cultural landscape today is less than a century old, it is not particularly thrilling to study features with which we are already familiar. The older and more subtle elements of the Pembrokeshire landscape are those which we can discover with excitement and study with enjoyment. I have had a long love affair with Pembrokeshire, and I have tried to explain my fascination -- and my obsession -- through the pages of this book.

Brian John

October 1999

SECTION ONE: FEATURES OF THE NATURAL LANDSCAPE

North Pembrokeshire is a region of immensely ancient rocks. Most of these are of Lower Palaeozoic age, more than 395 million years old. In three areas (around St. David's, in the Talbenny - Johnston - Burton area; and in the Hayscastle - Roch - Treffgarne Gorge area) there are volcanic and intrusive rocks of Precambrian age, more than 1,000 million years old. Generally these rocks are not associated with spectacular landscape features, but the bleak windswept Treffgarne Ridge owes its origin to the resistance of what geologists term the "Roch Rhyolitic Series". Exposures of flinty rhyolite may be seen in the narrow constriction at the north end of Treffgarne Gorge, and in the crags of Roch Castle,

Plumstone Rock, Poll Carn and Maiden Castle. The photograph below shows the fragile tor of Maiden Castle, seen from the south-east. Naturally enough, the

silhouette of the crags has given rise to local reference to "the family of lions". Nearby is the well known Lion Rock.
Further reading: 1,3,4

**1 Maiden Castle (955248)
The oldest rocks in Wales**

2 Lydstep Haven (099987)
The younger rocks of South Pembrokeshire

The southern part of the county is made of rocks which are for the most part between 395 million and 250 million years old. They are referred to by geologists as "Younger Palaeozoic rocks", but they are still old by comparison with most of the rocks of southern Britain. Where Carboniferous Limestone outcrops on the south Pembrokeshire coast, it gives rise to spectacular and beautiful cliff scenery, with steep cliffs, stacks, arches and caves in abundance. Some of the best known limestone cliff scenery is to be found between Flimston and Stackpole Quay, on Lydstep Headland, and on Caldey Island. This photo shows the cliffs of Proud Giltar in Lydstep Haven.
Further reading: 1,3,4,5

All around the coasts of North Pembrokeshire we can see evidence of the immense forces that have built -- and destroyed -- the great mountain ranges of the past. The ancient rocks of Precambrian, Cambrian and Ordovician age have been bent and buckled, tilted on edge, and shattered by faulting on many occasions. Much of the deformation of these rock layers occurred during the "Caledonian" earth-movements, which created a vast mountain range some 450 million years ago. Most of this range has now been denuded to such an extent that all we see in Pembrokeshire are the undulating hills of Mynydd Preseli and the structures in the "stumps" of the

**3 Ceibwr, near Moylgrove (110460)
Forces that built mountains**

original mountains, revealed in the coastal cliffs. The more recent rocks exposed around the South Pembrokeshire coast have also been folded and faulted, about 250 million years ago during the "Hercynian" mountain-building episode. This photo shows the tight folds in the cliffs near Ceibwr. *Further reading: 4,5*

The spectacular clifftop platform of south Pembrokeshire was probably formed in the Tertiary period, when sea-level was substantially higher than it is at present. Sea-level was falling intermittently, but every time there was a prolonged "stillstand" a new erosion surface was cut by wave action on the coast. Only the lowest, or youngest, of these surfaces are today clearly preserved, for the higher ones have been largely destroyed by river processes. The superb coastal platform of the Castlemartin Peninsula was cut by marine processes when sea-level was more than 125 feet

**4 Flimston Castles (930945)
The coastal platform**

higher than at present, relative to the land. It is difficult to date accurately, although there are some ancient deposits which show that it is more than 35 million years old. The present shoreline has been established more or less in its present position only within the last two million years. The photograph shows the clifftop erosion surface at Flimston Castles. This complicated limestone peninsula is riddled with caves, chasms and arches.
Further reading: 3,4

The undulating uplands of Mynydd Preseli attain an altitude of only 1760 ft, but here on the south-western fringes of Great Britain exposure has given them a bleak windswept beauty. Bedrock is for the most part shale and mudstone of Ordovician age, which has weathered easily to form smooth gentle slopes ideal for hill walking. The outlines of the uplands were probably complete before the onset of the Ice Age; however, the effects of long periods of cold climate can be seen in the smooth mantles of frost-shattered material which lie over many of the slopes. Glaciation has changed the landscape relatively little, but at least once during the Ice Age the immense Irish Sea glacier over-rode the Preseli Hills. This can be shown by the manner in which trails of "erratic" boulders have been transported by the ice towards the lowlands of the south and south-east from the uplands. The photograph shows the northern flank of the main upland ridge, seen from near Brynberian. *Further reading: 3,4,5*

5 Preseli Hills near Brynberian (085340)
The uplands of Pembrokeshire

6 Cwm Gwaun (063353)
Landscape change in the Ice Age

Opposite: During the geological period of the Pleistocene (commonly called the Ice Age), Pembrokeshire was inundated on at least two occasions by the ice of the Irish Sea Glacier. The ice did not come down from the mountains, but in from the sea, flowing from NW to SE. During the earlier of these two glaciations the glacier probably extended as far as Wiltshire and as far south as the Scilly Isles. At the end of this glaciation, about 100;000 years ago, vast quantities of meltwater were produced; in the area around Fishguard, Trecwn and the Gwaun Valley this meltwater eroded a spectacular series of channels. These are called "subglacial meltwater channels", because the meltwater which eroded them was flowing under great pressure far beneath the downwasting ice surface. Under these conditions certain sections of the channels were cut by meltwater actually flowing uphill. The photograph shows the beautiful wooded Gwaun Valley near Llanerch. *Further reading: 3,4,5*

**7 Carnedd Meibion Owen (093362)
Later traces of glacier action**

Above: During the last glacial episode, which finished about 13,000 years ago, only the northern and western coastal fringes of Pembrokeshire were affected by glacier ice. The precise position of the ice edge at the time of its greatest extent (around 18,000 years ago) is still a matter of dispute. However, there are abundant traces of ice action in the county, including striations or scratches made by tools on the bed of the glacier, smoothed bedrock surfaces (for example, on Carnllidi near St David's, on Garn Fawr near Dinas, and on Carningli near Newport), till or boulder-clay around the coast, and sands and gravels laid down by torrents of water during the wastage of the glacier. The photograph shows a "perched" erratic block on an ice-smoothed rock surface at Cerrig Meibion Arthur near Brynberian. *Further reading: 3,4,5*

**8 Carn Meini (145326) and Stonehenge
   The bluestone enigma**

Opposite: In the Preseli uplands there are many magnificent "carns" or tors which add jagged detail to the generally smooth hill slopes. Several of these carns have featured in a heated debate between geologists and archaeologists. It has been known for many years that some of the "bluestones" in the incomplete inner circle at Stonehenge came from Pembrokeshire, and authorities have made much of the fact that the three main types of bluestone (namely, dolerite, rhyolite and volcanic ash) occur naturally close together in a small area in the Preseli Hills around Carn Meini. This has given rise to a widespread and romantic belief that the builders of Stonehenge deliberately transported stones (some of which weighed more than 5 tons) from this area, probably because they considered the locality sacred. Some say that a whole "Preseli Stonehenge" was transported by men, stone by stone, across land and sea, to Salisbury Plain. The theory of the transport of the bluestones, described in most detail by HH Thomas and R

Atkinson, has both been enthusiastically endorsed and strongly criticised. Recent writers have pointed out that:

1. The Stonehenge bluestones do not all come from the Preseli Hills, but from localities in both upland and lowland Pembrokeshire. Some are not from Pembrokeshire at all.

2. The original Stonehenge bluestone circle may have had 80 stones, and it is likely that more than 50 of these were not "foreign" at all.

3. There is no firm archaeological or other evidence for the transport of the bluestones by man, although a small-scale BBC experiment in 1954 proved that it was possible to move large stones with rollers and rafts.

4. The "human transport" theory was put forward before the discovery of glacial deposits east of Bristol and Bath. Accordingly, the Irish Sea Glacier could have carried the bluestones from Pembrokeshire and across the Bristol Channel to Somerset and even Wiltshire.

The debate continues, but much more evidence is required before one or the other of the debating parties can feel vindicated. The main photograph opposite shows the crags of Carn Meini. The inset photograph on this page shows two bluestones in the "inner bluestone horseshoe" at Stonehenge.

Further reading: 5,27,40

9 Cliffs near Dale (790062)
Cliffs and coves

cliff scenery cannot all have been created in this short period of time (geologically speaking!), so we must assume that much of our coastline is very old, being freshened up by wave action whenever the sea happens to be at a convenient level. There is a substantial amount of marine erosion going on at present in Pembrokeshire, since ours is a "storm wave" or high-energy environment. Cliff falls are frequent, and sometimes there are coastal landslides and slumps. Caves are being excavated; arches are formed and destroyed; and wave-cut platforms are being extended as the coast retreats under the inexorable battering of the waves. Many of the details of the coastline are related to local geology. Headlands and peninsulas almost always coincide with hard or compact rocks, while creeks, coves and bays are created by the sea where the rocks are soft or broken by faulting and folding. The photograph shows an area of jagged stacks and reefs on the Old Red Sandstone coast near Dale. *Further reading: 3,4,5*

During the Ice Age sea level has oscillated violently in response to changes in global climate. About 80,000 years ago it was higher than at present, but during the last glacial episode it sank at least 100 feet in response to the huge volumes of water locked into the world's ice sheets. With ice melting, it returned to more or less its present level about 7,000 years ago. Pembrokeshire's

The Green Bridge of Wales is one of the landscape "icons" of Wales, and photographs of it have been reproduced in countless publications. It is nonetheless beautiful for all that. The famous natural arch, seen here from the west, has been formed by the coalescence of two caves from opposite sides of an old headland. The arch now has a height of about 80 feet, and at its narrowest point the apex is only 4 feet wide. Nearby are Stack Rocks and their seabird colonies, and the limestone coastline between Linney Head and Stackpole Head is justly famous among students of coastal geomorphology. Because limestone is susceptible to both chemical and mechanical erosion, the

10 **The Green Bridge of Wales (925944)**
The destruction of the coast

coastline here features solution hollows and blowholes, caves, arches, stacks, overhangs, steep-sided clefts, rockfalls and gullies filled with shattered rock fragments and ancient red soils. *Further reading: 1,3,4*

Before and after each of the glaciations of the Ice Age there were periods of cold climate, when Pembrokeshire experienced "periglacial" conditions similar to those of Iceland or Spitsbergen at the present day. In this climate of low temperatures, strong winds and heavy snowfalls, only a low "tundra" vegetation of shrubs, grasses, mosses and herbs could survive. There were no trees. The ground was probably frozen for the greater part of each year, with frost action shattering the bedrock. Where cliffs or crags were exposed to the atmosphere, blocks were broken off by frost to fall and

**11 Mynydd Carningli (063372)
The work of frost**

accumulate as scree at the foot of the slope. These deposits can occasionally still be seen beneath steep slopes inland, and on the coast one may see exposures of coarse frost-shattered rubble called "head", which has accumulated to thicknesses of 50 ft or more. The angular stones in head can move downslope on quite gentle gradients as a result of a slow process called "solifluction". In Pembrokeshire one can find traces of several different phases of periglacial climate, but the shattered stones on the upper flanks of Carningli date from the time of the last glacial episode which ended some 10,500 years ago. The scree slope surface here is still unstable, and the continuing downslope movement of broken stones accounts for the lack of surface vegetation.
Further reading: 3,4,64

The natural harbour of Milford Haven has been considered by many as one of the finest deep-water anchorages in the world. It is some eleven miles from the Haven mouth to Mill Bay, at which point it swings northwards to the Daugleddau (the common estuary of the rivers Cleddau). Almost as far inland as Neyland the Haven maintains a width of about one mile., and allows access to vessels of up to 55 ft draught at all states of the tide. Silting is not a severe problem, and the only real disadvantage of the waterway is its entrance, which is relatively shallow and exposed to the prevailing south-westerly swell. These factors contributed to the "Sea Empress"

disaster in February 1996. The branching pattern of Milford Haven and its tributary tidal creeks demonstrates a fluvial origin. It is a "ria", or drowned river system similar to those of southern Ireland and the south coasts of Devon and Cornwall. It was cut when sea-level

was at least 100 ft lower than at present, possibly before or during the early part of the Ice Age. This photograph was taken from the Cleddau Bridge, looking westwards towards the Texaco Refinery. *Further reading: 3,4,69*

**12 Milford Haven Waterway (970045)
A drowned river valley**

13 Coast near St Ann's Head (804027)
The western coasts

There is magnificent cliff scenery around the three shores of St Bride's Bay and on the west-facing coasts of the St David's Peninsula and the Dale Peninsula. In places the coast is wild and forbidding, especially where it is assaulted by the full force of the Atlantic waves. Some of the cliffs on Ramsey island are over 350 feet high. Elsewhere, as on the south shore of St Bride's bay, more sheltered conditions are associated with gentler and lower cliffs. The stretch between Ramsey Sound and Newgale typifies the character of this region; the gently undulating farmland of the St David's Peninsula is truncated by rugged cliffs which make up in colour and grandeur for their lack of height. Tiny coastal inlets such as Solva and Porthclais are all but hidden from both sea and land. Almost without exception the bays and inlets are cut in soft shales and other sedimentary rocks, while the headlands are of igneous rock or hard sandstones. On the outer coast near St Ann's Head red sandstones and marls give the cliffs a typical and unique colouring. *Further reading: 2,3,4,72*

Newgale pebble-beach, about 1.5 miles long, is one of the most spectacular coastal features of the county. It has been constructed by storm waves to a height of some 17 ft above the sandy beach on its seaward flank. At high tide during severe storm conditions, pebbles are thrown by waves over the crest of the ridge and on to the A487 road, which runs behind it for part of its length. The storm beach has been built here in the north-east corner of St. Bride's Bay because the coast is assaulted by "high energy" waves from the southwest. Most of the stones in the beach are of local grey, green and blue sandstones from the St. David's Peninsula, but there are also many far-travelled glacial erratics. Probably the beach has been built from glacial deposits on the floor of St. Bride's Bay; wave action has gradually driven them eastward and concentrated the larger pebbles during the gradual rise of sea-level during the last 10,000 years. This photograph shows Newgale pebble-beach, seen from the north. Before it is the impressive sweep of Newgale Sands, and behind it is the dammed valley of Brandy Brook.
Further reading: 3,4

14 Newgale Pebble Beach (846223)
Coastal construction

15 Broomhill Burrows (934000)
The work of the wind

Beach. There are many areas of sand dunes at the heads of smaller coastal embayments also. Most of the dunes were built thousands of years ago, and they have long since been stabilised by vegetation. However, the sand dune environment is a delicate one, and in several popular holiday areas the destruction of the thin vegetation cover has allowed the wind to excavate "blow-outs". These steep-sided hollows may be 50 feet deep, and if allowed to grow they could alter the whole character of some of our most attractive coastal areas. The photograph: shows part of the sand dune complex of Broomhill Burrows, at the head of Freshwater West beach. Here the dune vegetation is relatively undisturbed, but nevertheless large amounts of sand are blown inland by onshore winds. *Further reading: 3,4,6*

Some of the wide sandy beaches of Pembrokeshire have provided ample material for the wind to carry inland and build into sand dunes. Large areas of dunes exist at Whitesands Bay (Tywyn), Freshwater West (Broomhill, Kilpaison and Gupton Burrows), the Teifi Estuary (Towyn Warren), and Tenby South

The tidal mud flats of the Daugleddau estuary are largely responsible for the fascinating character of this part of the National Park. Wide expanses of mud and stones are exposed during every tow tide in the arms of the Western Cleddau and Eastern Cleddau, the Cresswell and Carew Rivers and several small "pills". Outside the National Park the Pembroke River has similar mudflats, and further west the flats of Angle Bay and Gann Flat (Dale Roads) lie in the coast section of the Park. Since these flats extend from the mouth of Milford Haven to the tidal limit at Haverfordwest they are subject to a wide range of conditions. Those flats furthest inland may be affected by a tidal range of up to 26 feet, and by waters which are not nearly so saline as those in the Haven proper. Similarly, the speed of tidal streams varies from place to place, as does water temperature and turbulence. As a result of these factors a wide variety of environments occurs on the different mud flats, making them attractive to many species of wild fowl. This photograph was taken on the Carew River at low tide. *Further reading: 3,4,6*

16 Carew River (040040)
A tidal estuary

The climate of Pembrokeshire has a profound influence upon the landscape, for it determines which trees and plants can survive. Similarly it affects soil formation, and exerts a powerful control over patterns of agriculture. Oceanic influences are dominant, and mild moist weather conditions penetrate through the whole of the county. At St. Ann's Head temperatures fall below freezing-point only on some three or four nights per year; for ten months the average monthly temperature is above 7 degrees C, allowing almost unbroken plant growth. Thus spring arrives very early and autumn is protracted; cattle and sheep can be kept out of doors throughout the year. While the climate is as mild as that of South Devon and Cornwall, day-to-day weather is often characterised by alternating short sunny spells and cloudy spells with showers. On the coast there

17 Wind-bent tree on Dinas Island (013410)
The climate of the present day

may be over 1800 hours of sunshine per annum and only 31" of rainfall; but inland the climate deteriorates rapidly, and the Preseli Hills receive over 60" of rainfall annually. Trees find it difficult to establish themselves in the uplands, and even more difficult on the coast as a result of exposure to high winds and salt spray. St. Ann's Head is assaulted by an average of 31 gales each year, and there are many records of wind velocities over 100 mph. If the Pembrokeshire climate is considered mild by meteorologists, it is considered somewhat draughty by the locals. The photograph shows a wind-sculpted tree on a clifftop on Dinas Island. The winds that have affected this tree have been blowing upslope from the north and the east. Cliff faces appear to have a "accelerating" or "suction" effect on onshore winds.
Further reading: 3,4,5

Visitors who come to Pembrokeshire in May and June are frequently amazed by the wild profusion of flowering plants which they find on the clifftops. Quite literally, the colours have to be seen to be believed. In the early spring there are snowdrops and primroses in sheltered spots, and white scurvy grass, purple violets and blue spring squill on clifftops blasted by gales and drenched by salt spray. Later, on the clifftops, there are banks and cushions of thrift or sea-pink, cascades of white sea campion, prickly thickets of gorse glowing rich yellow and smelling of coconut oil, delicate ox-eye daisies, and prostrate broom on rock faces. Even daffodils survive in some coastal locations, and the sheets of bluebells on Skomer are justly famous. The coastal heath vegetation is in a delicate state of balance, and can be damaged by human feet and grazing animals. There are currently a number of clifftop management schemes in progress; one of them is intended to protect the short-cropped grass which is essential for the wellbeing of the Pembrokeshire chough population. This photo shows healthy cushions of thrift on the west side of Skomer Island. *Further reading: 5,6,66,72*

18 Skomer Island (725087)
The clifftop flower garden

19 Tycanol Wood, near Newport (090370)
Ancient woodlands

Most of the ancient woodland of Pembrokeshire has disappeared, trampled underfoot by the inexorable march of progress. Forest clearance has been going on since the Iron Age; and although Pembrokeshire may appear superficially to be a well-wooded county most of the mature deciduous trees that survive are in very small copses or in old hedgerows. Genuine old woodlands are few and far between. Luckily, some of the surviving old woods are now protected by designations as Sites of Special Scientific Interest, and they have management plans in place to ensure that they are not threatened by building development or even by heavy levels of recreational use. Tycanol Wood, located between Newport and Brynberian, is a very special oak wood which has probably never been totally cleared even though it has been used for meeting local timber requirements down through the centuries. The oak trees in the wood are gnarled and twisted, and many of them are shallowly rooted on the flanks of rocky crags and cliffs.
Further reading: 4,6

Our most ancient ancestors used whatever shelter they could find, for they were hardly capable of any modification of the natural environment with the simple tools at their disposal. Some of the earliest homes of man in Pembrokeshire have been found in coastal caves. During the last glaciation, sea-level stood much lower than at present because vast amounts of moisture were locked up in the world's ice sheets. For thousands of years the offshore zone of south Pembrokeshire was dry land, vegetated by tundra plants and inhabited by herds of reindeer, mammoth, wolves and other cold-climate animals. Upper Palaeolithic man is known to have occupied caves on Caldey Island, in the St. Govan's area,

**20 Hoyle's Mouth Cave, near Penally (113003)
The home of early man**

and on the Gower Peninsula. At present many of these caves are inaccessible except by a precarious roped descent of the cliff face. However, the cave at Hoyle's Mouth (seen in this photo) is easily reached by a scramble through the woods; although it is now more than a mile inland, at the time of its occupation it looked down on the shore of a wide treeless valley which no doubt provided good hunting.

Further reading: 5,40,66

21 Mynydd Caregog (053366) The upland heaths

On the commons of Mynydd Preseli, Mynydd Carningli and Mynydd Dinas there is a type of dry heath vegetation which is at its most beautiful in the month of August. This is when the dry grasslands are at their best, with yellows, browns and ochres replacing the lush greens of spring and early summer. But most spectacular are the great expanses of purple heather and golden gorse, blooming together under the late summer sun. On the lower slopes there are large areas of bracken, hated by farmers and animals but bringing a rusty hue to the landscape once the days begin to shorten. The management of these commons is crucial both for grazing animals and for ground-nesting birds, and the feudal institutions called Court Leets have a key role to play, for example in controlling the size of the grazing sheep flock. Many commons are burnt each spring by the farmers, and this prevents gorse from taking over the grazing areas as well as keeping heather and bracken under control.

Further reading: 5,6,33,64

SECTION TWO: THE EVOLUTION OF THE MAN-MADE LANDSCAPE

22 Pentre Ifan Burial Chamber (100370)
The Neolithic settlement

About 5,500 years ago the Neolithic people arrived in West Wales, probably by means of skin-covered boats. They usually settled within sight of the sea, and cleared some forest by burning. Probably they also practised a simple form of shifting cultivation. These people have left few traces of their occupation of the landscape; but their memorials are the megalithic monuments which are scattered throughout the county. These are called dolmens, or "cromlechau" in Welsh. The structures which we see today are simply the massive stone interiors of earth burial chambers; the mounds that flanked and sometimes over-topped them have been removed by erosion and by the hand of man. Pentre Ifan cromlech is located not far from Nevern. It is in a lovely setting.

Certainly it is one of the most spectacular megalithic monuments in the country, with a spectacular south-facing forecourt and with a capstone measuring almost 17 feet by 10 feet supported by three tall pillars. At some stage the structure formed the core of a "long barrow" 135 feet long and 35 feet broad, whose outline can still be traced.
Further reading: 11,40,65

**23 Foel Drygarn, near Crymych (157337)
Bronze Age burial mound**

were made with copper and bronze, and trading activity (for example between South-East Ireland and Pembrokeshire) increased. The most interesting landscape features dating from the Bronze Age are perhaps the old circular enclosures, hut sites and field boundaries on Mynydd Carningli near Newport, but there are many other round barrows, embanked stone circles, and cist graves elsewhere in the county. By far the most spectacular of the local Bronze Age features are the three massive drystone burial cairns perched on the summit of Foel Drygarn near Crymych. One of these is seen in the photograph. *Further reading: 27,40,66*

About 4,000 years ago the "age of stone" gradually gave way to the "age of metal". People became more sedentary; their communities grew larger; and they began to make quite sophisticated pottery. Weapons, tools and ornaments

Bronze Age people seem not to have maintained an interest in building large "megalithic" structures out of stone. Perhaps this was because, following the invention of metal axes and knives, timber structures were easier to build, and perhaps there were changes in their religious beliefs and social organization. But they were still enthusiastic in the matter of erecting tall standing stones, and 3,000 years ago there must have been thousands of them all over Pembrokeshire. Most have been removed for use as gateposts or incorporated into hedge banks, but many still remain, especially in the north of the county. The majority stand alone, but there are some pairs and some alignments. Many of them mark ritual sites, but some may have been territorial markers, waymarks or even cattle scratching posts. The most famous "twinned" stones are located in the amphitheatre of Cwm Cerwyn, and are called Cerrig Meibion Arthur. They are, according to legend, the grave markers of two of the sons of King Arthur who fell in battle, but archaeologists now think that they may mark a Bronze Age fertility ritual site. One of the best-known standing stones in Pembrokeshire is Bedd Morris, near Newport. It stands on the crest of the upland ridge between the town and the hamlet of Pontfaen. There are a number of legends about it, the most familiar being the sad tale of a duel between two young men for the hand of the fair maid of Pontfaen. She loved the one called Morris, and he was the one who died in the duel. He was apparently buried at this spot (the name means "the grave of Morris"), and after his death the fair maid died of a broken heart. Such is the stuff of legends....
Further reading: 27,40,66

24 Bedd Morris (037365)
The old standing stones

There is only one stone circle in Pembrokeshire, located on a beautiful open stretch of moorland south of the village of Mynachlogddu. It is easily accessible from a nearby minor road. The Gors Fawr circle is not very impressive, since none of its 16 stones is more than three feet high, and they are not even set in a perfect circle. However, the site is very romantic, with the jagged crests of Carn Meini on the skyline to the north, and this has led many enthusiasts to the conclusion that the circle was placed here, around 5,000 years ago, because of its close proximity to the "sacred mountain". Others believe that the Stonehenge bluestones were also originally set up in an ancient stone circle somewhere in the vicinity, and were then taken down and transported across the sea and far away. As far as Gors Fawr is concerned, archaeologists refer to it as a "ritual monument" without specifying what this means. The photograph shows the stones of the circle with the Preseli upland ridge in the background. *Further reading: 5,40,66*

25 Gors Fawr, near Mynachlogddu (135294)
A stone circle

During the later part of the Bronze Age, about 3,000 years ago, the climate deteriorated somewhat, and the Celtic immigrants of the Iron Age had to contend with cool, damp conditions. Nevertheless, the density of their settlements was greater than that of any of their predecessors and it is they who must have been largely responsible for the removal of much of the virgin forest. Their homesteads were often established within earth ramparts and ditches located on either clifftop headlands or easily defended hillocks or river bluffs inland. The earliest forts were protected by single curved banks, but by 100 B.C. double curved embankments were being built. Probably there were massive timber stockades on top of the banks. Families lived on platforms inside the fortifications, their crude stone dwellings covered with a lattice of branches and thatched with bracken, rushes or turf. Remains of Iron Age houses are not common, but promontory forts occur on all the coasts of Pembrokeshire. Inland there are the great hill forts at Garn Fawr, Mynydd Carningli, and Foeldrygarn, and many more forts are marked on the map as "raths" or "camps". This plate shows the site of a small promontory fort on the shore of Ramsey Sound. *Further reading: 5,26,40*

**26 Promontory Fort at Castell Heinif (723248)
Traces of Iron Age settlement**

The settlers of the Iron Age obtained their food from domestic cattle, pigs and sheep, from wild animals caught in hunting, and from fish and shellfish obtained in streams and in the sea. They collected nuts and berries, fruit and wild honey, but depended to a great extent upon the growing of grain. Methods of agriculture were more efficient than during the Bronze Age, and iron agricultural tools were manufactured on a large scale. As part of the economy small irregular fields were made close to sites of prolonged settlement, defined by rough stone walls. These fields were used for protecting growing crops from cattle and sheep, and also for the enclosure of livestock, which must have been an important form of wealth. Most traces of these ancient Celtic field systems have long since been eradicated, but small irregular fields still exist in many parts of north Pembrokeshire, and many

"modern" field boundaries may in fact be over 2,000 years old. On the flanks of Carningli, below a substantial Iron Age defended settlement site, there are wonderfully preserved enclosures and paddocks, hut circles and stonewalled passages, as seen in these two photos.
Further reading: 5,27,40,64

27 Carningli, near Newport (063372)
Hut circles, enclosures and early agriculture

After 400 AD many Christian missionaries arrived in Pembrokeshire and began the work of converting the pagan Celtic tribes. Most of the holy men of the Celtic Church held a strong belief in individual monasticism. Consequently a network of small religious cells was set up throughout the Welsh tribal territories. Some of these cells attracted later settlement, but some were so remote, and located in such unfriendly sites, that they have long since been abandoned and forgotten. The photograph shows St. Govan's chapel, wedged precariously into a cleft in south Pembrokeshire's limestone cliffs. The rock-cut cell and the altar and bench hewn from stone probably date from a simple 5th century building, but most of the structure to be seen today is no older than the 11th century. Perhaps inevitably, St. Govan's has its own hermit legends and its own Holy Well. One of the legends associates the locality with Sir Gawain, one of the Knights of the Round Table said to have turned hermit after Arthur's death.
Further reading: 26,40,71

28 St Govan's Chapel (966930)
Monastic cells

29 Nevern Celtic Cross (083400)
The Age of the Saints

As the centuries passed Pembrokeshire became the centre of a thriving Christian community, being located at the crossing of two major sea-routes. One of these ran between the Bristol Channel and Ireland, and the other between the South-West Peninsula and the Isle of Man. In addition to the isolated religious cells built by mystics and ascetics, small churches for the use of the growing Christian congregation were built all over the county. During the later part of the Dark Ages church dedications were often associated with religious "cults". The cult of St. Brynach was based for the most part upon north Pembrokeshire. Nine churches are dedicated to the saint, all on or near the ancient pilgrim route that ran westwards towards St David's. The photograph shows the famous ornately-inscribed Celtic Cross in Nevern Churchyard, which probably dates from the early 11th Century. It stands 13 feet high. Also in St. Brynach's Church are three stones inscribed with the ancient Ogham alphabet; at least two of these date from the sixth century. *Further reading: 5,8,32,40,71*

Opposite: St David's, which prides itself on being the smallest city in Britain, is the site of the most famous cathedral in.Wales. The church of St. David probably began in the secluded valley of the River Alan as a monastic cell, about the year 520 A.D. However, as the reputation of the founder grew so did his church and its settlement, then called Menevia. On at least three occasions the cathedral was destroyed during the period of Norse raiding between 800 and 1100 AD -- in spite of the fact that it was completely hidden from the sea. The present structure was commenced in 1180, but several centuries of work under a succession of Bishops was needed before the building assumed something like its present form. In the Middle Ages the cathedral was renowned throughout the British Isles, in spite of its remoteness from the main centres of population. Two pilgrimages to the shrine of the Patron Saint of Wales equalled one to Rome. The photograph shows the Cathedral in its wooded hollow, seen from near the ford of the River Alun.
Further reading: 8,24,39,61

30 St David's (751254)
The Cathedral of the Patron Saint

**31 Skomer Island (722088)
The coming of the Vikings**

keeping close to the sheltered waters of Milford Haven. Perhaps because Viking buildings were of wood, no traces remain of this occupation; but some authorities claim that it is supported by documentary evidence, by blood-group affinities with southern Scandinavia, and by the frequency of place-names of Norse derivation -- for example Hubberston,

One thousand years ago Pembrokeshire people lived in fear of the Vikings. Over a period of three hundred years Scandinavian raiders ravaged the coastal settlements over and again. In one period of only ninety years St. David's was burnt eight times and two Bishops were killed. Even hilltop settlements such as Mathry suffered greatly at the hands of the pirates. Eventually the Vikings are thought to have established temporary or seasonal settlements in the south and centre of the county, moving inland from favourable coastal sites but Ramsey, Grassholm, Skokholm, Musselwick, Goskar, and Caldey. Skomer Island (seen in this photo) was well known to the Viking seafarers. The name is derived from "Skalmey" which means "island with a cleft or fissure".
Further reading: 5,8,10,26,72

The Norman armies arrived in Pembrokeshire in 1093 and quickly conquered the south of the county. The first Pembroke Castle, built of "stakes and turf", was established at a strategic and easily defended site on a rocky peninsula, flanked by two of the inlets of the Pembroke River. The castle was rebuilt in stone by Gerald of Windsor in 1105, but its present form is largely the creation of William Marshall and his five sons between the years 1189 and 1245. Situated in the heart of the developing Anglo-Norman colony and easily accessible by sea from Milford Haven, Pembroke was for 300 years or more the chief fortress of "Little England". From it, the Earls of Pembroke initiated a transformation of the south Pembrokeshire landscape; there was intensive settlement under the feudal system, and at least 120 new manorial villages were established in the countryside. This photograph shows the massive stone keep and some of the defences of the inner ward. *Further reading: 8,40,45,66*

32 Pembroke Castle (982016)
The Norman Conquest

Soon after the Norman conquest of South Pembrokeshire, it became apparent that fortresses were needed to defend the new colony against the Welsh chieftains, who combined forces for a series of damaging raids from the north. Accordingly a chain of castles was constructed across the county from St. Bride's Bay to Carmarthen Bay. The main links in this chain were the castles at Roch, Wiston, Llawhaden, Narberth and Amroth. Of these, Wiston and Narberth Castles are largely destroyed and the present Amroth Castle is a late 18th century replacement of the original structure. No stone castle was ever built in the vicinity of the deep wooded Treffgarne Gorge, which had a medieval reputation as a haunt of Welsh robbers. The "frontier castle" at Roch is still in an excellent state of repair. Its high peel tower, built in the thirteenth century, is visible for many miles around. It was owned by the Roche family until 1420. After the Civil War the castle was deserted for over 200 years, but it was restored in 1900 and has been further improved since then. For some years it has been used for self-catering holidays. *Further reading: 5,16,40,45*

**33 Roch Castle (880212)
The fortification of the Landsker**

Opposite: The Bishop's lands of the St. David's Peninsula and central Pembrokeshire escaped many of the effects of the Anglo-Norman colonisation. Nevertheless, the invaders soon ensured that Normans occupied the Bishop's throne, and as the centuries passed they became in effect powerful feudal lords, accustomed to living in some style. By 1500 there were bishop's palaces at St. David's, Llawhaden and Lamphey. The bishops also held seven manors. As landlords they gave much and demanded much of their tenants. Lamphey Palace is, in its ruinous state, still a place of great beauty and tranquillity. Within the precinct wall we can see a fine inner gatehouse, two large halls, a chapel, courtyards, and residential quarters. Excavations have shown that there were stables, bakehouses, storerooms and brewing houses. In 1326 there was a walled garden, a deer park, two water mills, a windmill, a dovecote, orchards and fishponds. In 1507 the palace was the scene of entertainment on the grand style, with the bishop heavily involved in the "Last Great Tournament" organized for a thousand guests by Sir Rhys ap Thomas at nearby Carew Castle. *Further reading: 29,40,41,61*

34 Lamphey Palace (019009)
The Bishop's southern palace

During the medieval period the main towns of the Englishry (Pembroke, Haverfordwest and Tenby) were strongly fortified, and much of their early growth took place within the town walls. In itself, this is a sign of the pressure under which the colonists felt themselves, and there are frequent records of savage Welsh raids into the new Anglo Norman colony. As more peaceful times arrived, the towns spread beyond their original confines, and in many places the walls with their battlemented towers have been destroyed to make way for later developments. Small remnants of the town walls can still be seen in Pembroke and Haverfordwest, but Tenby has the finest sections still standing. The walls were probably built in the late thirteenth century, although some enlargements and embellishments, particularly to the gatehouses, are as late as the fifteenth and sixteenth centuries. Unfortunately the seaward defences and three of the old gates have now disappeared. This photograph shows the South Gate, whose five arches permit access to the town's main shopping area. The gatehouse is a Tenby icon, and neither residents nor visitors would do without it. *Further reading: 22,40,45*

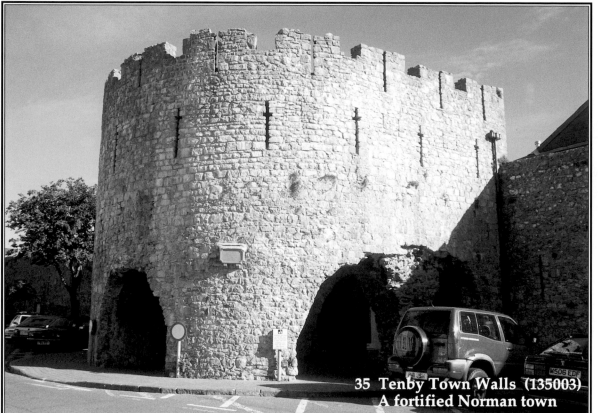

**35 Tenby Town Walls (135003)
A fortified Norman town**

36 Plumstone Rock (916234)
The Landsker -- the invisible
frontier

When the Normans built their line of "frontier castles" across the county, they may have thought of it as defining the northern edge of their new colony. But they soon changed their minds, and individual knights pressed northwards with colonising zeal up into the foothills of Mynydd Preseli. They established new villages in Letterston, Puncheston, Little Newcastle, Ambleston, New Moat, and Henry's Moat, and they even established a new barony on the north coast with its headquarters in Newport. But these new settlements did not attract large-scale immigration, and they managed to retain part of their Welsh-speaking population. Gradually an invisible cultural divide called "The Landsker" came into being. During the fourteenth century it was a sharp economic, linguistic and social divide between the Englishry and the Welshry, and this situation persisted until well after 1600. Times have changed, and now of course there are no major differences in land holding systems or agricultural practices between the two regions of the County.

But the Landsker (as a language divide) can still be traced with ease by anyone who wishes to try. Its position across mid-Pembrokeshire has been remarkably stable for more than 300 years, and the section which runs from Newgale to Roch and through Plumstone Rock to Treffgarne is the most stable of all.
Further reading: 5,45

37 Llanwnda Church (932397)
The churches of the Welshry

Opposite: Most of the immigrants who came to Pembrokeshire during the twelfth, thirteenth and fourteenth centuries were settled on the manors of the Englishry. To the north of the Landsker Welsh tribal life continued in a modified form, and even where manors were established there was incomplete acculturation of the local population. Welsh traditions and language survived, as indicated by place name, architectural and historical evidence. The cultural geography of the Welshry still shows many distinctive characteristics, including the frequency of simple "Celtic" church-types. These churches often have small bellcote towers, a rectangular plan and plain interior decoration. They are often located in isolated places, and were built to serve small communities of farmers who can never have been particularly prosperous. The church at Llanwnda is a well-known example of a "Celtic" type church, in a spectacular location close to the coast of Pencaer. *Further reading: 5,41,44,61*

38 Carew Cheriton Church (045028)
The building of the Norman churches

During the period of Anglo-Norman colonisation in the south of the county many new churches were constructed. Generally they were built to meet the defensive as well as the religious needs of new communities; this is demonstrated by their disproportionately high battlemented towers. The main church buildings which can be seen today are often of more recent date than the towers. Church interiors are occasionally ornate, as a result of extensive renovation particularly in the late 1800's. The churches are not truly "Norman" in architectural style; they are more imposing and more elaborate than their counterparts to the north of the Landsker because they were built to serve prosperous village communities rather than dispersed farming communities. The photograph shows the impressive church at Carew Cheriton, not far from Carew Castle. The massive tower was, and is, a truly intimidating "statement" on Norman wealth and power. *Further reading: 17,40,44*

The early part of the Middle Ages saw a growing interest in monasticism, and abbeys and priories were built on a number of new sites under the patronage of the Norman feudal lords. These new religious houses were much more elaborate than the little "clas" establishments built by the adherents of the Celtic Church, and the communities which they housed were much more organized. They were not only important as centres for spreading the gospel. They also fed the starving, helped the poor, healed the sick, and developed agriculture. The Cistercian order was particularly successful in Wales, with its emphasis on asceticism, labour and rural simplicity. In Pembrokeshire the main religious houses were at St Dogmaels

**39 Priory Ruins, Haverfordwest (956152)
The religious houses**

(a Tironensian abbey), Haverfordwest (an Augustinian priory), Pill near Milford Haven (a dependent priory of St Dogmaels) and Caldey (originally a Celtic community, then a dependent priory of St Dogmaels, then a Benedictine abbey, and now a Cistercian abbey). There were other smaller religious houses too, for example at St David's, St Non's, Llawhaden, Whitewell, Monkton and Slebech. Caldey is the only place where the monastic tradition has been maintained more or less continuously to the present day, but there are numerous relics of the "monastic" era in the landscape. The photograph shows part of Haverfordwest Priory, now rescued from further decay by a major archaeological investigation and refurbishment project.
Further reading: 34,40,43,61

Pembrokeshire is full of ancient tracks, which can be found if you know where to look. One of the oldest is the "Golden Road" which runs along the crest of the main ridge of Mynydd Preseli. It is probably a trading route established by Bronze Age people and used more or less continuously for the last 5,000 years. Many of the standing stones of the county may also mark ancient routeways. As the years passed more and more footpaths and bridleways were opened up, and many of these were maintained as "traditional" routes even after the enclosure of much of the old common land took place. The drovers had many routes of their own, used to drive herds of cattle, geese, sheep and pigs from the Pembrokeshire collecting points to the

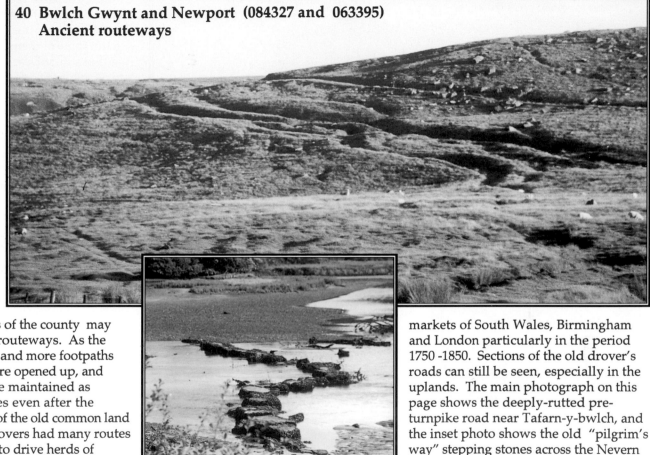

40 Bwlch Gwynt and Newport (084327 and 063395) Ancient routeways

markets of South Wales, Birmingham and London particularly in the period 1750 -1850. Sections of the old drover's roads can still be seen, especially in the uplands. The main photograph on this page shows the deeply-rutted pre-turnpike road near Tafarn-y-bwlch, and the inset photo shows the old "pilgrim's way" stepping stones across the Nevern River near Newport.
Further reading: 8,33,40,52,66

**41 "Flemish Chimney" at Rhosson
(729253)
Medieval building styles**

Chimney experts recognise three types of medieval domestic chimneys in Pembrokeshire. Most of them were square; some of them were cylindrical like those in St David's Bishop's Palace and Monkton Old Hall; and others were conical or tapering. Farmhouses with massive conical chimneys were at one time common in Pembrokeshire, but now few remain. Most of these are in the St. David's area. They were built in the fifteenth and sixteenth centuries, and demonstrate the adaption of castle building techniques to the requirements of domestic architecture. Generally these dwellings were occupied by husbandmen or yeomen, and were more solid and elaborate than the cottages of labourers and poor craftsmen. While round chimneys are generally referred to as "Flemish" chimneys in Pembrokeshire, there is no evidence that they were either built by Flemings or that their distribution coincides with the area of medieval Flemish settlement. The photograph shows the famous round chimney on the old farmhouse at Rhosson, adjacent to the St David's and St Justinian's road.
Further reading: 24,40,48,61

The Tudor period was a time of great prosperity in Pembrokeshire, and the fact that Henry Tudor had been born in Pembroke Castle and had started his march to Bosworth Field from the county led to a broad support for the English crown even among the Welsh-speaking community. During the 1500's conditions were -- for most of the time -- relatively peaceful. Great strides were made in agriculture and commerce, and even a few small "industrial" activities were started up. Much of the new economic activity was controlled by the powerful gentry families, with Sir John Perrot of Haroldston involved in politics, trade and piracy in equal measure. But now a new and dynamic merchant class began to appear. Many of the merchants were shipowners who used their vessels to export cloth, timber, fleeces, grain and other commodities and to import salt, fruit, ironware,

cheese, wine, flour, and a wide range of luxury items into the Pembrokeshire ports -- particularly Haverfordwest, Tenby and Pembroke. Markets were thriving and the medieval guilds were still powerful. As they made their money from buying and selling., many of the merchants built fine houses. Sadly, hardly any of them remain in good condition, but the Tudor Merchant's House in Tenby (seen in this photograph) is a little gem. It is tucked away down a little alley, between Tudor Square and the harbour.
Further reading: 22,40,49

42 The Tudor Merchant's House, Tenby (137003) The Elizabethan era

Sailing vessels have been made around the Pembrokeshire coast for thousands of years, but prior to the Tudor period there were few communities which actually specialised in boat building. But with the vast increase in coastal trading activities in the sixteenth century professional shipbuilders became valuable members of the coastal communities, and they attracted other skilled craftsmen also -- for example sail-makers, specialist blacksmiths, rope-makers, tanners and chandlers. Haverfordwest, Tenby, and Pembroke had semi-permanent shipyards which

**43 Lawrenny Quay (017065)
Sailing ships and shipwrights**

provided local merchants with the trading vessels they needed. Later on larger shipyards were built at Milford and Neyland, with the Royal Naval Dockyard at Pembroke Dock bringing a new scale and sophistication to the industry. But the little yards in places like Dale, Newport, Saundersfoot and Solva were family affairs. There were few permanent fixtures or fittings, and ships would simply be built on sheltered beaches just above high water mark. Thousands of little ships were built, and thousands have sunk or have rotted away. A few relics remain, like this one near Lawrenny Quay.
Further reading: 5,7,8,64

Pembrokeshire people have been grinding things up with mechanical power for well over 3,000 years, but it was during the Middle Ages that water power and wind power began to be harnessed on a substantial scale to serve the needs of the feudal communities that were springing up in the lowlands and the uplands. Watermills were the easiest to build, and almost every manor in the county had at least one for the production of flour. But there were also windmills in St David's, Tenby, Lamphey and elsewhere. Twr y Felin, which dominates the city of St David's while the cathedral hides away in its little valley, is the best known of the old windmill towers. In the eighteenth and nineteenth centuries many more flour mills were built in the countryside where the energy of fast-flowing streams could be tapped. Most of the small mills served the farming community; but others were built on private estates, and some in the towns (such as Cartlett Mill and Prendergast Mill in Haverfordwest) were associated

**44 Blackpool Mill (060145)
Corn, furze and bone mills**

with sawmilling and manufacturing businesses. Some of the little mills on the farms of the uplands were used specifically for the milling of furze of gorse, which was an essential winter animal feedstuff. There were two tidal mills, one at Carew and the other in the shadow of Pembroke Castle. The latter

was destroyed by fire in 1956, and the former stopped work after a phase of bonemeal production which almost shook the building to pieces! The large mill at Blackpool, seen in this plate, was built in 1813 and ground wheat and barley for local farmers until the 1950's. *Further reading: 5,15,59*

**45 Porthclais (743237)
Trading from the little ports**

served as bases for local traders dealing in such commodities as agricultural produce, coal, kelp, ale, cloth and livestock. Small sailing vessels were occasionally built in temporary shipyards. Even the smallest communities were proud of their maritime traditions, and trading contacts were maintained with the main Pembrokeshire ports of Haverfordwest, Pembroke and Tenby, with Devon and Cornwall, Bristol, the Irish ports and even the coast of Brittany. The era of the coastal trading ships came to an end with the completion of the county's railway network, although some vessels continued to trade spasmodically until the early 1900's. The photograph shows the little harbour at Porthclais, used for trading and fishing for over 5,000 years, and now used largely for recreation.
Further reading: 5,48,62

From the later medieval period until the middle of the nineteenth century many vessels from the small ports and harbours of Pembrokeshire's outer coast participated in coastal trade. There were flourishing little ports at St Dogmaels, Newport, Fishguard, Porthclais, Solva, and Abercastle, and within the Milford Haven Waterway there were quays at Dale, Lawrenny, Llangwm, Carew, Cresswell, Landshipping and other localities. They

During the 1600's the landed gentry of Pembrokeshire wielded considerable influence in the fortunes of the community. There were many fine estates, some descended from the manors of the Anglo-Norman period and others built up, bit by bit, by successful trading families who wished to climb the social ladder. Among the older estates can be counted Picton, Orielton, Wiston, Prendergast, Slebech and Boulston. Their families enjoyed a life of ease, refinement and affluence, although as a result of intense rivalry between them some prospered at the expense of others as one generation succeeded another. In the eighteenth and nineteenth centuries there were frequent lavish entertainments at the various stately homes, and many of the more affluent families participated each winter in the London "season". Haverfordwest became a fashionable centre with many fine town houses, and later Tenby and Broad Haven became well known as watering-places. The fine house at Bush was the home of the Meyrick family. It was rebuilt in 1906 following a fire, and it is now used as a residential home for the elderly.

Further reading: 20,29,51,61

46 Bush House, near Pembroke (979025)
Stately homes and high society

Right: In the centre of Pembrokeshire Haverfordwest was established in pre-Norman times at the lowest bridging point and head of navigation on the Western Cleddau river. Most of its early growth was, however, associated with the Anglo-Norman settlement. In the Middle Ages it was first an important strategic centre with its impressive stone fortress and town walls, and later a service centre for the growing agricultural community of the county. Its markets became important, and it thrived upon industry and trade. There were guilds of feltmakers, glovers, saddlers, tailors, carpenters, tanners, and blacksmiths, and flour milling and paper making were important. During the sixteenth century the town acquired the administrative functions of chief town of the county at the expense of Pembroke, which henceforth declined. The Flemish settlers in the centre of the county were probably responsible for the town's merchant traditions, and through a combination of factors it became one of the chief ports of Wales, maintaining a flourishing trade with British and overseas ports. Relics of this era of sea-borne trade can be seen in the two quays which line the western bank of the river in the town, the dilapidated warehouses

47 Haverfordwest
(956153)
The rise of the
merchant class

and custom house, and other old buildings in Quay Street and Bridge Street.
Further reading: 5,14,34,43,68

Opposite: While it may be unwise to generalise about the form of Welsh "peasant" cottages, they do have several features in common. In Pembrokeshire many of the simple cottages which survive from the eighteenth century are rectangular in plan, with a central door and only two rooms. The smaller cottages have no upstairs rooms, although there may be a small loft. However, interior walls, ceilings and stone floors have only become common within the last century. Fireplaces and chimneys are generally located at the gable ends. Thatch roofing was originally widespread, but within the last century there has been an increasing use of stone slabs or slate, perhaps covered with a cement wash. Cottages built of "clom" (a mixture of clay and shale fragments) were once common, particularly on the Pembrokeshire coalfield; but now few of them survive. The same may be said of the medieval and later cottages built with mud walls, although these primitive dwellings were still widespread in the county a century ago. The photograph shows a simple cottage at Treleddyd-fawr, near St David's, with colour-washed clom walls and a typical cement-washed roof. *Further reading: 24,28,40,48,66*

48 Treleddyd -fawr (753278)
The Welsh cottage

Milford Haven (which is always locally referred to simply as Milford) is a new town in exactly the same sense as Hemel Hempstead, or Bracknell, or Killingworth. It was planned and laid out on its grid-iron base largely as a result of the energy of Charles Greville, who induced a colony of refugee Nantucket Quakers to become the first settlers. After the founding of the town in 1793 the Quakers soon abandoned their whaling activities, and the hopes of the community turned to manufacturing and trading. There were visions of Milford Docks as both a shipbuilding centre and a transatlantic passenger terminus, but plans never materialised and the real growth of the town after 1904 was based upon the fishing industry. The lay-out of the town is readily apparent to the visitor, as is the consistent architectural style of many of the older buildings. Links with the past can be seen in St. Katherine's Church (built in 1801 - 1808 by Charles Greville), the Observatory at Hakin and the Friends' Meeting House near the town centre. Place-name evidence for the major influences upon the town's early growth is abundant; Hamilton Terrace, the Lord Nelson Hotel, Dartmouth Gardens, and Charles Street are but four examples of sites with obvious historical associations. As shown in this photograph, Milford has several wide, attractive streets and pleasing garden areas. This is Charles Street, the commercial core of the modern town. *Further reading: 26,30,31*

49 Milford (905058)
A 'new town' of the
Eighteenth Century

Pembroke Dock was the second of the new towns to appear on the shores of Milford Haven. It grew after 1814, when plans were made for a new naval dockyard at Paterchurch. As the dockyard grew so did the town, with its planned grid-iron layout and its well designed public amenities. The Irish packet service was transferred from Milford to Pembroke Dock in 1836, and by the 1850's the dockyard was a hive of activity. As a result of the disturbed political situation on the continent, Milford Haven assumed some strategic importance, and a military garrison was established at Pembroke Dock. The railway arrived in 1864, and for the rest of the century the town prospered, its fortunes based upon both civilian and naval shipbuilding. There was employment for some 3,000 men. During the boom years many famous vessels were built here, including the "Tartarus" of 1834 (the first steam man-of-war) and the "Conflict" of 1846 (the first warship with a screw propeller). Three royal yachts were built, and there were many naval barques, brigantines, cruisers, gunboats and battleships. During the Great War the Dockyard specialised in the building of small, swift cruisers. In all, more than 250 naval vessels were

built here. In 1926 the Admiralty abruptly closed the Dockyard. As the unemployment rate approached 25% the borough was classed as a Distressed Area. The population declined. During the Second World War attempts were made to resurrect the town by the establishment of an RAF Sunderland flying-boat base and a naval base, and there was repair and construction work in the dockyard. But the naval base closed

in 1946 and the flying-boat base in 1958. Recently the dockyard has been modified through the provision of a new deep-water basin, new quays, and warehouses with cold storage facilities. The "Port of Pembroke" is currently undergoing further change, with new access roads and facilities for the Irish Ferries terminal. The photograph shows two of the old Dockyard buildings. *Further reading: 5,14,26,36,46,55*

50 Pembroke Dockyard (963037)
Relics of the shipbuilding industry

After the period of Anglo-Norman settlement, the strategic importance of Milford Haven appears to have passed unnoticed until Thomas Cromwell stressed the need for survey and fortification in 1539. During the later part of the sixteenth century two blockhouses were constructed on either side of the Haven entrance but there is no record that they were effectively used for the defence of the waterway. The building of the Naval Dockyard at Pembroke Dock gave the deep water anchorage much greater strategic importance, and in the period 1820 -1860 many elaborate plans were put forward for the fortification of the Haven. Five forts were built near the mouth of the harbour, another four in the vicinity of the town of Milford, and four (including a Defensible Barracks) around Pembroke Dock. Others included a fort at Scoveston (completed in 1865), designed

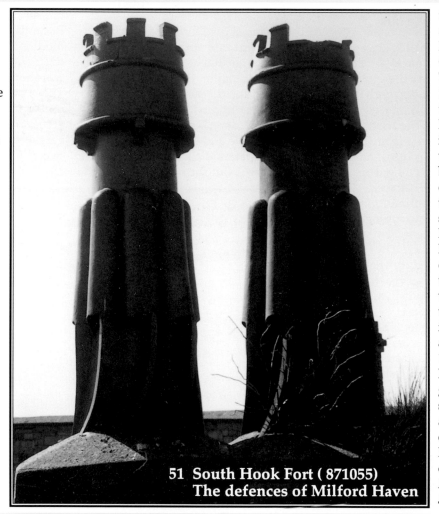

51 South Hook Fort (871055)
The defences of Milford Haven

to defend the landward approaches to the Haven, and St. Catherine's Fort at Tenby (completed in 1875), designed to defend the Castlemartin Peninsula. Several other inland and coastal forts were planned but never built. Of the forts which can still be seen around the shores of the Haven, some (such as the Popton Point Fort and the Hubberston Point Fort) could accommodate more than 200 soldiers and were armed with more than 25 guns. In all, the forts could accommodate a total garrison of about 1900 men, defending the Haven with 220 heavy guns. The photograph shows two of the tall and heroic chimney pots on the roof of South Hook Fort, inside the old Esso Refinery site. *Further reading: 8,26, 36,46,55*

The second half of the nineteenth century saw the growth of Pembrokeshire's rail network. In 1849 the South Wales Railway reached Haverfordwest, and with Brunel as engineer it was extended to the north shore of Milford Haven by 1856. Here the town of "New Milford" (Neyland) was created on a wing and a prayer, and those who settled there prayed that the port would become a great transatlantic terminus. In the event it enjoyed a brief period of prosperity as a fishing port and as the packet port for Ireland. There was even some shipbuilding. But the passenger vessels moved to Fishguard in 1906; the fish trade died and the wagon works closed in the same year. In 1965 the railway line from Johnston to Neyland was itself closed, and in 1971 the track was lifted. For some years there was a Technical College in Neyland, and prior to the building of the Cleddau Bridge a little vehicle ferry shuttled across the waterway, come hell or high water, between Neyland the Hobb's Point. The "Cleddau Queen" and "Cleddau King" won quite a place in the affections of Pembrokeshire people. But then, with the passage of the first vehicle over the bridge, the ferry became redundant. Later, with the opening of the grand new Pembrokeshire College in Haverfordwest, Neyland "Tech" closed too. Now the little town finds itself increasingly isolated, by-passed by traffic using the Cleddau Bridge and with inadequate commercial facilities. However, the old rail terminus has been transformed by a successful marina and chandlery. Small businesses based upon fishing and other maritime activities have been attracted to the Brunel Quay Business Park, and good-quality "waterfront" housing has also proved popular especially among leisure craft owners. *Further reading:* 5,8,36,66

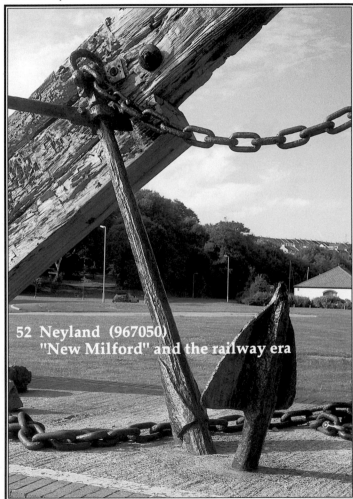

52 Neyland (967050) "New Milford" and the railway era

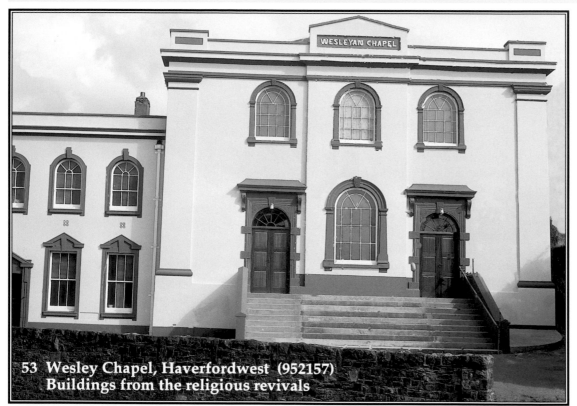

**53 Wesley Chapel, Haverfordwest (952157)
Buildings from the religious revivals**

built with the subscriptions of ordinary people rather than with the endowments of the landed gentry. Most of the local chapels were built during the religious revivals of the eighteenth and nineteenth centuries, when enthusiasm among non-conformist congregations was at its height. Methodist, Baptist, Congregational and Presbyterian congregations enlarged and restored their churches frequently during the 1800's, and it is not uncommon to find three or four non-conformist chapels close together providing a total accommodation for some 3,000 worshippers. Now, however, congregations are much reduced, and many of the smaller country chapels have been forced to close. The photograph shows the ornate and colourful Wesley Chapel in Haverfordwest, prior to its sale and conversion into an architectural salvage store. It was one of three large non-conformist buildings close to the Norman parish church of St. Martin.
Further reading: 5,34,41,43

The non-conformist chapels of Pembrokeshire are important elements of the landscape. Generally they conform to a simple rectangular design, although there may be additional buildings which serve as schoolrooms and vestries. In country districts the chapels may have their own adjacent graveyards, but in towns this association is rare. Chapel exteriors are plain and Gothic in style, although they are occasionally brightly painted. For the most part they were

The Coal Measures in Pembrokeshire extend in a broad belt across the centre of the county from St. Bride's Bay to Carmarthen Bay. Seams of anthracite are close to the surface, but are folded and shattered. Coal was mined in the county before 1500, particularly near Roch and in the Kilgetty-Jeffreston area, but it was not until 1800 that the coalfield attained national importance. Annual production reached a peak of 146,000 tons in 1865, and it was said that Queen Victoria was so pleased with the cleanliness and burning efficiency of Pembrokeshire coal that she would use nothing else in the boiler rooms of her royal yachts. But as the nineteenth century progressed there was a gradual decline in production, and mining operations finally came to an end in 1948. There are at least 140 abandoned mines on the coalfield, for the most part in the two major mining districts of Daugleddau and Saundersfoot Bay. The coal was exported from small quays such as Little Milford, Hook and Landshipping, from the larger quays at Llangwm Pool and Lawrenny, and from Saundersfoot Harbour. The small quays are now largely destroyed, and one has to search hard to find traces of the old mines. Here and there one can see subsidence pits and hummocky terrain where old spoil tips have been scavenged and then left to nature. At the southern end of Newgale beach, and in the Settlands at Broad Haven and around Little Haven, there are old mining tunnels in the cliffs. Saundersfoot Harbour is a coal industry "relic", as are the little railway tunnels around Coppet Hall. On balance, Pembrokeshire's short-lived Industrial Revolution has left little except memories. The photograph shows one of the few traces of the coal industry near Newgale. The old engine room stack of the Trefrane Cliff Colliery is being eaten away by salt spray.
Further reading:
5,8,15,26,53

54 Trefrane Cliff Colliery (856197)
Pembrokeshire's coal industry

**55   Abereiddi "Blue Lagoon" (795315)
Quarrying for slate**

There is a long history of quarrying in the county. Apart from small-scale quarrying of building stone to meet the needs of local communities, slate and shale flags became increasingly important for roofing and flooring purposes after 1800. Limestone was also quarried on a substantial scale, both for the production of building stone and for lime burning. The "slate" quarry at Abereiddi was worked most intensively in the latter part of the nineteenth century, when slates were exported not only to the rest of the county but also to the Bristol Channel and English Channel ports. Small vessels could be loaded at Abereiddi, but because of its exposure it was unsuitable for the larger vessels. Consequently most slate was hauled by narrow-gauge railway along the valley side to Porthgain harbour for export. The quarry closed in 1904. The photograph shows the flooded quarry pit, and its narrow entrance from the sea. It is now used only as a harbour for pleasure craft and small fishing boats, and it is a popular diving locality. Nearby are the derelict quarry buildings, traces of the old railway, and the remains of a row of quarrymen's cottages.
Further reading: 8,42,53,62

The success of the local coal industry encouraged the establishment of two ironworks in the Saundersfoot area. The most important of these was at Stepaside, opened in 1849. It used locally mined anthracite (from the Grove Colliery) and iron ore taken from the cliffs between Coppet Hall and Wiseman's Bridge; the tunnels into the cliffs can still be seen adjacent to the track of the old mineral railway. Limestone from nearby quarries was also used. By 1864 the Ironworks was exporting 3,000 tons of pig iron annually from Saundersfoot Harbour, and much iron was used by local industries. There were also substantial exports of iron ore, particularly during periods when the furnaces were not "in blast". In the national depression after 1873 smelting operations were forced to cease, but a workshop was

maintained at the Ironworks until 1929. The second works was close to Wiseman's Bridge. It opened in 1850 and operated until 1924, specialising in castings and a wide variety of other metal goods for colliery plant, ships and agricultural machinery. Some of the buildings of the Stepaside Ironworks, including lime kilns, beam engine shed and railway sidings, can still be seen. The photograph shows the remains of the casting shed.
Further reading: 5,8,38

56 Stepaside Iron Works (140075)
Iron-working in the county

A fascinating relic of industrial activity in north Pembrokeshire can be seen at Porthgain on the Cardigan Bay coast, some seven miles from St. David's. There were two quarries, one used for stone and the other for slate. Crushed igneous rock was being exported from the small harbour before 1878 by Porthgain Village Industries Ltd. The stone crushing plant was built for the most part with bricks made on the spot from local shale. The company ran a fleet of six specially built steam coasters, each displacing about 350 tons, and in addition sailing ships called regularly for the export of stone and slate from the Porthgain Quarries and from Abereiddy. Between 1902 and 1904 a new harbour with larger quays was built, and business was brisk until 1914. In just three months in 1909, for example, 12,897 tons of crushed and graded stone were exported in 101 shipments from the harbour to the ports of South Wales, South-West England, and as far afield as London and Essex. In the same period the large brickworks was in full production, and approximately 200,000 bricks were exported. However, the Porthgain Company found it increasingly difficult to make profits in the recession years following the Great War, and it was forced to cease operations altogether in 1931. The photograph shows the remains of the smithy buildings on the clifftop near the stone quarry. *Further reading: 5,8,62,26*

57 Porthgain (814327)
The rise and fall of a coastal port

The middle of the seventeenth century saw many small harbours in use around the Pembrokeshire sea coast. Solva Harbour was the best on St. Bride's Bay, although its difficult entrance retarded its development. Among its exports were timber, corn and other agricultural products, and small coastal vessels imported coal, culm, cloth and luxury goods from Bristol, the Irish ports and further afield. In 1851 Solva was a thriving community, and there were at least nine warehouses in Lower Solva. However, before 1860 the village, like most of the other small coastal settlements of the county, saw a decline in its trading functions as a result of competition from Pembrokeshire's new railway network. The photograph shows the harbour as it is today, populated largely by leisure craft.
Further reading: 5,24,13,53

**58 Solva Harbour (803242)
Trade on the open coast**

59 Shiphill Limekiln, Newport (063397)
The lime burning industry

Lime has been burnt in Pembrokeshire for at least a thousand years. Initially kilns were used for the production of mortar and whitewash for castle building and embellishment, but later it was discovered that dressings of slaked lime could be used to counteract the acidity of local soils, and by 1600 lime was in widespread use as a fertiliser. Hundreds of limekilns were built around the coast, some of them in remote creeks and at the head of exposed open beaches. The main ports and harbours all had clusters of kilns; there were once twelve in operation at Solva, eleven in Haverfordwest, and seventeen in Tenby including two clusters at Kiln Park. The western cluster at Kiln Park is particularly impressive, and is reputed to have been designed by the architect John Nash. It contains a drive-through tunnel within which rows of horses and carts could load with lime from the draw-holes. The kilns all used Pembrokeshire anthracite and crushed limestone from the South Pembrokeshire quarries, and the need for a constant supply of feedstock fuelled a large volume of coastal trade by little merchant vessels. The last Pembrokeshire kiln stopped operating in 1948, and now the kilns, of various designs, are nothing more than fascinating coastal relics. *Further reading: 5,12,33,64*

Slates from the Rosebush Quarries have been used on the roofs of Pembrokeshire houses for hundreds of years, and were even chosen for the roof of the Palace of Westminster. The newer slate quarries close to the village were operating in the middle 1800's, and as demand for roofing slates grew the Narberth Road and Maenclochog Railway was built in 1876 in order to provide easy export facilities. The line somehow attracted sufficient passenger traffic to encourage six years of development at Rosebush Station. The quarry owners financed the excavation of artificial lakes which were stocked with fish. A coach service to Fishguard was inaugurated, stables were built adjacent to the station. and the Prescelly Hotel was built to accommodate tourists. Extensions were carried out in the quarry, and twenty-six cottages

were built for the workers. Tourists were expected to flock in by rail, and considerable sums were spent on advertising the attractions of the hills. By 1880 the population of Rosebush had risen to 179 persons. After a series of financial escapades the line was linked to Fishguard in 1899, but it was badly constructed and enjoyed only short prosperity. In 1906 the direct line from Haverfordwest to Fishguard was opened,

and Rosebush became a backwater overnight. The slate quarries closed, and later the whole railway track was lifted during the First World War. By 1923 the G.W.R. (who now owned the line) had re-laid the track again, and further attempts were made to attract tourist traffic. Unfortunately in spite of energetic advertising, no more than 50-100 passengers a week could be induced to use the line, and passenger services ceased again in 1937. In 1949 the last goods train ran on the North Pembrokeshire branch, and in 1952 all of the track was lifted. The photograph shows the steps of the main quarry pit; visitors can still see the quarry buildings, the old station, the quarrymens' row, the ornamental gardens, the managers office, and the famous corrugated iron hotel (now named Tafarn Sinc). *Further reading: 5,8,18,63*

60 Rosebush slate quarry (080301)
The Rosebush saga

**61 Milford Docks (900057)
Milford's fishing industry**

Milford developed largely by accident into an important fishing town. After the completion of the Docks in 1888 a small local fishing industry established itself, and as the value of the western fishing grounds was realised more and more trawlers and drifters used the port.

Between 1900 and 1914 there was a remarkable growth of the Milford fleet, which rose from a strength of 66 trawlers and 150 smacks (in 1904) to become the basis of the town's economy. At the beginning of the Great War almost 2,000 people were engaged in the fishing industry. The fish market was expanded and more dock facilities were built. After the inevitable slump of 1914 - 1918 there was a rapid recovery, and a record landing of 46,000 tons of fish was made in 1920. Milford was now in the top league of fishing ports, but between the wars annual catches fluctuated violently and over-fishing of the western grounds was evident by 1931. The 1939-45 War allowed the fishing grounds to be rested, and led to a short-lived moment of glory; in 1946 the catch rose to a record 59,286 tons, with over 100 trawlers operating from the Docks. Milford occupied fourth place in the fishing league, after Grimsby, Hull and Fleetwood. However, since 1950 the decline of the fishing industry has been spectacular, caused by over-fishing and rising costs. In 1991 the last of the local trawler companies went into liquidation. Nowadays only a few trawlers use the Docks, and some of these are registered in Spain. There is an ice-provision service and an electronic fish auction, but much of the catch nowadays is trans-shipped straight to the continent in heavy lorries. The photograph shows one of the oldest buildings at the docks, originally used for the storage of whale oil and now converted to house the town's Museum. *Further reading: 5,30,31,53*

Before the Second World War housing conditions in Pembrokeshire were generally considered to be unsatisfactory. In the period 1919 -39 only 775 houses were built by the local authorities; most of these were in the urban areas, and the rural authorities were largely unaware of the need to provide adequate housing in order to prevent depopulation of the countryside. During the war estates of small asbestos "prefabs" were built in several towns; although they were intended to be temporary they proved to be very popular, cheap to maintain, and resistant to wear and tear. In the post-war period there was an energetic programme of council house construction, and blocks of pleasant council-owned "semis" and terraces sprang up in both towns and villages. Between 1946 and 1952 no less than 2,248 council houses were completed in the county; Haverfordwest Rural District led the way with 615 houses within its own

62 Riverside Avenue, Hakin (896060)
Post-war council housing

area. Since 1960 many large housing estates have been built by private enterprise, particularly in the urban areas where population increases have been most rapid and where much sub-standard housing has been demolished to make way for commercial and other developments. The photograph shows part of a post-war council estate in Hakin; here most of the properties have been sold off, and owners have "personalised" their homes through redecoration schemes, new windows and other modifications.

Further reading: 5,30,68

63 Goodwick Station (945383)
The decline of the railways

The railway network of Pembrokeshire was completed in 1906 with the construction of the link between Clarbeston Road and Letterston junction. Although the link could only be built to double-track standards as far north as Manorowen, it enabled traffic from South Wales to reach Fishguard Harbour direct, thus by-passing the North Pembroke and Fishguard railway through the Preseli foothills. After 1906 all of the boat-trains used the new line. Since 1930 there have been several modifications of the rail network. In the Letterston area a branch line was run at the beginning of the Second World War from the old junction to the R.N. Armaments Depot at Trecwn, and other rail links were added in the 1960's in association with the growth of Milford Haven as an oil port. But generally the pattern has been one of decline. The service to Letterston was discontinued in 1965, as was that from Johnston to Neyland. In recent decades there have been frequent worries about the future of the Tenby and Pembroke Dock line; it is still open, sustained largely by the summer tourist trade and by the presence of the Irish Ferries terminal in the old Royal Naval Dockyard. But rail privatisation has not improved the quality of the local rail service. This photograph shows the deserted station building at Goodwick, not far from Fishguard Harbour. *Further reading: 8,36,53,62*

Close to the village of Bosherston, the branching valley system which contains Bosherston Pools is a favourite spot with holidaymakers. The natural promontory between the two western pools was used by Iron Age man as a defensive encampment site. The camp is easily discernible on the ground, enclosed by formidable defences which include an inner mound and ditch, and three outer lines of banks and ditches. The defences enclose an area of some 5 acres at the end of the promontory. During the Iron Age the little valleys may have been occupied by arms of the sea, but today fresh water is impounded by an artificial dam and by the sand-dunes at the head of Broad Haven beach. The impounding work was undertaken around 1790 by the Earl of Cawdor as part of his "grand project" on the Stackpole Estate.

64 Bosherston Lily Pools (976960)
Landscapes of Leisure

Money was apparently no object, and the grandeur of the new Stackpole Court, with its 150 rooms, landscaped grounds and ancillary buildings, was the envy of the Pembrokeshire gentry. The longest arm of the pools is almost a mile long, and has two stone bridges. One of these is particularly spectacular, and has nine arches. That part of the "waterway system" most frequently visited by the public lies between the village of Bosherston and the lovely beach of Broad Haven. Three flimsy bridges carry the footpath across narrow sections of the pools, which are at their best during the early summer when the water lilies are in bloom. The photograph shows the long northern branch of the Lily Pools.

Further reading: 5,16,28,66

There was a little "folk industry" here, involving several families whose members collected a purple-brown "Porphyra" seaweed from the rocks between the tide marks for eventual transport to Swansea. The work on this exposed and storm-lashed beach was very hard, especially during the winter. Once gathered, the seaweed was spread on the draughty and sandy floors of the huts to dry, and it was then bagged up and sent by train from Pembroke station. In Swansea it was washed and cooked to make the peculiar Welsh delicacy called "bara lawr" or laver bread. The local industry faded away after the Second World War, but laver bread is still popular in the Swansea district. The thatched hut shown in this plate has recently been refurbished by the National Park Authority. *Further reading: 5,26*

65 Freshwater West (885994) Seaweed drying hut

On Little Furzenip peninsula overlooking Freshwater West beach there is a strange thatched hut. This is the last of the twenty or so seaweed drying huts that were built and looked after by the people of Angle in the period 1890 - 1940. The huts were very primitive, but they kept the rain off and allowed the wind to whistle between the rough planks nailed to the gable ends.

SECTION THREE: RECENT CHANGES IN THE LANDSCAPE

The farmed landscape of Pembrokeshire is currently undergoing a series of profound changes, linked partly to the recent crises in the food industry and partly to changes in farm support mechanisms. Farmers in the south of the county have something of an advantage over their neighbours in the north; their soils are relatively fertile, and with a climate that is less severe than that of the Preseli uplands, crops can grow for almost the whole year. Diversification in the arable sector is an option for many on lowland farms. Nevertheless, dairying is still the major source of income for local farmers, and much of the arable crop is still used as cattle feed. Some farms nowadays specialise on turkey breeding or pig breeding, and the recent farming crisis has encouraged other farmers to diversify into venison and ostrich meat

66 Farm near Scleddau (945326)
New crops for new markets

production, oilseed rape and maize growing, and even the production of industrial crops such as flax. In spite of the current crisis, there is still a strong demand for land which comes onto the market even in the more remote upland areas. This photograph shows a field of oilseed rape near Scleddau. Much of the crop is used in the food industry, but some oilseed varieties provide oil for industrial processes.
Further reading: 5, 56,59

67 Tregwynt Woollen Mill (894348)
The local woollen industry

The origins of the Pembrokeshire woollen industry are lost in the mists of history, but woollen cloth was certainly being woven on a small scale before the arrival of the Normans. Between 1300 and 1330 at least 71 fulling mills were established in Wales. Later on, many Flemish weavers arrived as refugees in the country, and they brought with them new skills. The Tudor woollen industry was home-based and disorganized, but nevertheless rough cloth was exported from the main towns. Later the industry declined, but after 1800 the invention of carding and spinning machinery allowed many small factories to produce woollen goods commercially. Most of the factories were water driven, and since they catered only for the local community they were not well located with respect to bigger markets. During the early 1900's there were at least 24 factories working in the county, but at present only two remain. They are located at Middle Mill (Solva) and Tregwynt (St. Nicholas). Tregwynt woollen factory is set in a pretty valley about a mile from the village of St Nicholas. There was probably a mill here in the Middle Ages, but the present buildings date largely from the nineteenth century. *Further reading: 5,16,37*

Pembrokeshire's rich heritage is now greatly valued, and there is a widespread conviction in the community that ancient relics are worth preserving. At Castell Henllys, near Eglwyswrw, an Iron Age village destroyed many centuries ago is actually being recreated. Most of the Iron Age settlements in exposed locations incorporated rather crude dwellings which were partly cut into the ground surface as "hut circles" and which had low roofs designed to cope with winter gales and lashing rain. However, in more sheltered locations such as Castell Henllys, some seven miles inland of Newport, substantial roundhouses with daub and wattle walls and conical thatched roofs were appropriate. The residents of this particular Celtic village invested huge amounts of labour in the construction of their dwellings, animal shelters and storage huts, and as a result were able to enjoy a standard of living far higher than that of the coastal or mountain tribes. The Castell Henllys Iron Age fortified settlement is still being investigated by archaeologists, but several fine huts have now been reconstructed on their original sites, and the National Park Authority has established an excellent "living history" centre for school groups and holiday visitors.

Further reading: 5,40,65,66

68 Castell Henllys (117390)
The heritage industry

**69 Merrion Camp (937970)
Military misuse of a National Park**

There are still three major military establishments in the county, at Castlemartin, Manorbier and Brawdy. The MoD land "holding" in the county is now reduced following the disposal of the mine depots at Trecwn and Newton Noyes. The Castlemartin tank range still occupies some 6,000 acres of land which was once renowned for its cereal production, and prevents open access to a magnificent stretch of limestone coast within the National Park. The presence of the camp is appreciated by the people of Pembroke and Pembroke Dock, for it brings in Army personnel who spend part of their free time, and part of their salaries, in the twin towns. But firing disturbs the peace of most of south Pembrokeshire, and there is a great deal of surface damage and scrap iron on the range. The range is grazed by sheep from the Preseli Hills during the winter months. The photograph shows Romulus, one of two retired tanks guarding the entrance to Merrion Camp. *Further reading: 26,50,66*

The natural assets of the Milford Haven water-way were recognized by the major oil companies in the mid-1950's, and in 1958 the decision was taken to develop it as a major oil port. The first refinery was built by Esso on the north shore of the Haven near Gelliswick. It was opened in November 1960, heralding the most important industrial phase in Pembrokeshire's history. Then came the Texaco refinery at Rhoscrowther (1964) and the Gulf refinery at Waterston (1968). Other important installations were the BP Angle Bay Ocean Terminal at Popton Point and its tank farm at Kilpaison, opened in 1960. The Amoco refinery near Milford, with a design capacity of some 4 million tons per annum, came on stream in 1973. Later the capacity of the Texaco refinery was expanded to about 9 million tons per year; and the Esso refinery

70 Texaco Oil Refinery at Eastington (875064)
The coming of the oil industry

pushed its production up to 15 million tons per year. By 1973 the refinery capacity of Milford Haven was about 34 million tons per annum. However, the heady days of oil industry expansion could not last, and a number of factors conspired to create difficulties for the local refineries. Esso, BP and Gulf have now all pulled out, and the old Amoco

refinery is run by Elf. The Texaco and Elf refineries are now modern and efficient, but with global over-capacity in oil refining they could be closed down at any moment. The photograph shows how the Texaco refinery dominates the old fortified house and farm at Eastington, near Rhoscrowther.
Further reading: 5,55,66,69

Large oil tankers are essential to the operations of the oil industry on Milford Haven. There are few anchorages in the British Isles which can accommodate vessels of over 150,000 tons; Milford Haven is one of them, for it has at least 55 feet of clear water at all states of the tide. Following the completion of a huge dredging and blasting scheme by the Milford Haven Conservancy Board in 1970, vessels of up to 255,000 tons could use the deep-water channel to the Esso, B.P. and Texaco jetties. The Gulf refinery jetty, being further up the Haven than the others, could not handle the largest supertankers, but it was adapted to accommodate vessels of 165,000 tons. As a result of the shipping associated with the oil industry, Milford Haven was, in the 1970's, easily the most important oil port in the British Isles, and was the nation's third-ranking port when seen in terms of cargo tonnages handled. Each of the refinery jetties was visited by more than 700 ships per annum, and there were over 7,000 shipping movements recorded each year for tankers and other large vessels. Now the level of activity is much reduced, and since North Sea oil is a major refinery feedstock fewer of the mammoth tankers use the port. The Esso refinery jetty, seen in this photograph, has not been used since the refinery was closed in 1983, and it is deteriorating fast. *Further reading:* 5,30,67

71 Esso jetty (875055)
The age of the supertanker

The CEGB Pembroke Power-station was completed in 1973 on the assumption that heavy oil residues would be available as fuel far into the future. It was built largely on reclaimed land in Pennar Gut, with most of the buildings on the site well screened by a ridge of Old Red Sandstone to the north. The 750 ft main chimney stack is somewhat difficult to hide! From the beginning the station received its oil by pipeline from the Texaco and Gulf refineries and from the B.P. tank farm, and had a capacity of 2,000 megawatts distributed between four 500 megawatt turbo-generators and boiler units. It was designed to burn 4 million tons of fuel oil per annum and to use 55 million gallons of seawater per hour for cooling purposes. But it hardly ever worked at full capacity. Almost from the beginning the power-station was a white elephant, and its fuel costs rose sharply as a result of international oil crises, more efficient refining techniques (which left fewer heavy oil residues for the power-station to burn) and the shift to lighter crude oils from the North Sea. By 1995 there were only 150 people working at the plant, and only one of the generator sets was in regular use. National Power (which took over following the privatisation of the electricity industry) sought to cut its losses by burning a cheap bitumen-based fuel called Orimulsion instead of fuel oil, but its planning applications were greeted with such a concerted campaign of opposition from local people that the plans were eventually dropped, and the power-station is now closed. The photograph shows the installation as seen from the south. The inset photograph shows one of the double row of gigantic pylons which carry the defunct 400 kV power lines from Pembroke towards Swansea. *Further reading: 5,55,66*

72 Pembroke Power-station (933027) Power from oil

73 St David's Visitor Centre (753253)
The Pembrokeshire Coast National Park

In recognition of the exceptional scenic qualities of much of Pembrokeshire, the National Park was designated in 1952. It covers over 250 square miles of countryside in four separate sections; the southern coast from Amroth to West Angle; the west coastal strip from St. Ann's Head to Llanwnda; the Preseli Hills section, including the coast between Fishguard Bay and Cemais Head; and the well-wooded tidal reaches of the Daugleddau waterway. Each of these areas has its own distinctive character, appreciated and enjoyed by about one million visitors each year.. Holiday developments and increased tourist popularity place many areas under pressure, and by 1970 many observers felt that the Amroth - Penally coastal strip was already over-developed. Careful planning is required if attractive settlements like St. David's and Newport are not to be spoilt. On the whole, many would judge that National Park planning has not been particularly successful in the county, and there is little doubt that in the outer reaches of Milford Haven the national interests of industry have prevailed over the local interests of amenity and conservation. However, things would have been far, far worse without the planning policies of the NPA. The preservation of beauty -- and the encouragement of sustainable economic activity -- will probably prove to be Pembrokeshire's key planning challenges of the next decade. *Further reading: 5,6,26,67*

Most holidaymakers who come to Pembrokeshire now have their own cars, and spend at least part of their holidays on wheels. But the magnificence of the rocky coastline cannot be fully appreciated unless one puts on one's sturdy footwear and takes to the coastal footpath. The National Trail, almost 200 miles long if you count in the headlands, runs from the Teifi estuary to Amroth. It was created or cleared by enthusiastic groups of volunteers working with few mechanical aids, and following its opening in 1970 it has become one of Pembrokeshire's prime holiday attractions. Its route is well marked on maps and in innumerable publications. "Circular" walks are possible for those who do not wish to walk more than 5 or 6 miles in a day. Most of the land traversed by the Coast Path is privately owned, and should be respected as such. The main photograph on this page shows a typical stile and finger-post on the

74 Coast Path near Dinas Fach (822232) The enjoyment of the coast

Coast Path between Newgale and Solva. The inset photo shows one of the more grotesque sections of the Coast Path, contained within a wire cage where it crosses the Gulf Refinery "pipe run" on the north shore of the Milford Haven waterway.
Further reading: 5,6,48,59,72

Pembrokeshire's holiday season has "stretched" in recent years, but it is still the case that the majority of visitors take their holidays between June and September. Holiday accommodation is now widely scattered throughout the county. Except in the Tenby-Saundersfoot area hotel accommodation is scarce, but many local people provide B&B facilities, and many small guest-houses have been opened. There has been a massive increase in the number of self-catering cottages available for rent. Caravan holidays are still popular, and there are currently about 12,000 static caravans on registered sites. However, no one would pretend that caravan sites enhance the beauty of the coastal area, and many of those permitted so far have been difficult to landscape effectively. In the more remote coastal areas caravan sites are now not

allowed at all, and future developments are to be concentrated inland. The photograph shows part of a large, popular and well planned caravan park

with excellent amenities at Kiln Park on the south side of Tenby. From it, there is easy access to the Golf Course and the South Beach. *Further reading: 5,22,26,59*

75 Caravans at Kiln Park, Tenby (125002)
The holiday industry

Since 1960 there has been a spectacular rise in the popularity of sailing in the county. In spite of the unpredictable nature of the local weather, the coast is relatively free of offshore shoals and rocks, and provides exhilarating sailing conditions. During the summer months regattas are held at the small coastal resorts of St. Bride's Bay, Cardigan Bay and Carmarthen Bay, and in the more sheltered waters of Milford Haven. As the oil industry has declined, the waterway has become a fast expanding centre for watersports, with several popular sailing clubs, two modern marinas at Neyland and Milford Docks, and watersports training based in the Cleddau Reach near Pembroke Dock. The photograph shows part of the Neyland marina facility adjacent to Brunel Quay. *Further reading: 5,26,53*

**76 Neyland Yacht Haven (968055)
The sailing boom**

77 Llysyfran Reservoir (037243)
Water supply and amenity

The industrialisation of Milford Haven led to a huge increase in the demand for water, met partly by new pumping station and flow regulation scheme on the Eastern Cleddau, and partly by a large-scale reservoir built at Llysyfran in the valley of the Afon Syfynwy. The concrete dam is 107 feet high, and has a total width of 1,100 feet. The reservoir itself is 1.5 miles long, and covers an area of 187 acres. It holds 2,000 million gallons of water, which is used to regulate the flow of the Afon Syfynwy. Up to 19 million gallons per day of industrial water can be abstracted. Because drinking water is not extracted direct from the reservoir, it is widely used for recreational purposes -- in particular sailing and fishing. Footpaths, car-parks and viewing points are provided for the public, and the Country Park also has an excellent visitor centre with a shop and restaurant. The photograph shows the concrete dam from the east.
Further reading: 5,6,56,63

**78 Pantmaenog Forest (083307)
Forestry in Pembrokeshire**

The first two decades after the Second World War saw much diversification of the rural economy, particularly in the uplands. As many of the small farms of the Preseli Hills closed down, extensive stands of trees were planted in their place. Afforestation meant that the uplands were being put to good use, but many local people still regret the loss of wild expanses of bleak moorland, and planting on roadsides which eliminated several fine views. In the last twenty years, the global oversupply of softwood, and falling timber prices, has caused many mature forestry plantations to fall derelict. The Forestry Commission has sold many of its small Pembrokeshire plantations. The Pantmaenog Forest, on the flanks of Mynydd Preseli, is being cleared, leaving behind scenes of dereliction and devastation. The photograph shows recently cleared forest land near Rosebush. *Further reading: 5,60,63*

Saundersfoot is a relatively modern village by Pembrokeshire standards, having grown along with the coal trade.

export via sailing ships which were loaded on the sandy beach. But in 1829 the harbour was built, and there was

and Wisemans Bridge. For a hundred years the harbour was used for the export of coal and culm, and (for a shorter period) pig iron and iron castings. Coal dust swirled about on the quays, and the beach is reputed to have been black rather than golden yellow. There was a little shipbuilding industry on the foreshore adjacent to The Strand, and there were also visits from fishing vessels and general cargo vessels. With the closure of the last local colliery in 1939 the harbour was given over to leisure craft, and it is now one of the most popular sailing centres on the Pembrokeshire coast. The adjacent beach is safe, shallow and easily accessible, and on summer days it is crammed with holidaymakers. *Further reading: 5,8,23,26,53*

**79 Saundersfoot Harbour (136005)
Tourism on the south coast**

By 1800 the little community was growing, with its inhabitants occupied largely with fishing, coal mining from primitive pits and coal and iron ore

great investment in the local coal and iron industries. New pits were sunk, railway lines were installed, and there were great developments in Stepaside

Many of the minor roads of Pembrokeshire date from the period of Norman and Anglo-Saxon settlements, but the major roads are largely products of the nineteenth century. Haverfordwest was an important collecting centre for cattle which were to be driven to English markets along the South Wales drover's roads, and these roads provided the first easy land contact between Pembrokeshire and the outside world. Later, the development of Milford Haven, Neyland, Fishguard and Pembroke Dock as ports led to the building of better roads for horse-drawn vehicles moving into and within the county.

80 **Dual carriageway in Haverfordwest (956157)**
The present-day road network

Haverfordwest benefited greatly from its position in the centre of Pembrokeshire, served by a radiating pattern of roads. During this century the rise of motor transport in the county has encouraged many improvements to the old road system, and the industrialisation of Milford Haven and the tourist "boom" have led to much increased traffic. During the summer months there is congestion in Haverfordwest and the coastal towns, and one-way traffic flows and by-pass schemes have proved essential. Most work in recent decades has been concentrated on the A40, A477 and A4076 trunk roads and on the link roads serving the Cleddau Bridge. The photograph shows a section of dual carriageway close to the town centre in Haverfordwest. *Further reading: 5,34,43,68*

**81 Cleddau Bridge
(975047)
The north-south
road link**

For many years the people of Pembrokeshire looked forward to a direct road link between the two shores of the Haven, since the lack of a linking bridge presented a severe barrier to social and economic integration between the main towns of the county. In the 1960's, with the industrial development of Milford Haven well under way, a box girder bridge was built across the waterway from Pembroke Ferry to Barnlake. Tragically there was a collapse of one of the sections of the bridge during construction in June 1970, and following an official investigation of box girder bridges the project was much delayed. The project was not completed until 1973, and the cost burden associated with it is still carried by the county council and the toll-paying users. The photo shows the bridge from Pembroke Ferry. *Further reading: 26,53,56,69*

Opposite: Since the decline of the Pembroke Dockyard and the Milford fishing industry, and the more recent decline of the local oil industry, the county (with substantial Government aid) has attempted to alleviate unemployment and diversify the economy through the establishment of small factories and business units available for letting to local firms. In this, the earliest success was achieved on the Thornton Industrial Estate near Milford. Subsequently small trading estates and business parks have been built all over the county, for example in Pembroke Dock, Haverfordwest, Goodwick, Tenby, Honeyborough near Neyland, Newport and Narberth. Some of these speculative projects have been successful; others are perceived as having been hugely wasteful of public funds. There are still worries about the high rate of unemployment in Pembrokeshire, and the county is included in the "Objective One" region designated for major EU financial aid. The photograph shows a new business unit under construction on a prime site adjacent to the southern end of the Cleddau Bridge; it is hoped that it will be used for a prestigious "call centre" development. *Further reading: 5,59,66*

82 East Llanion Business Park (976045)
   Present-day business facilities

In the early years of the new Millennium the size of the Pembrokeshire sheep and beef cattle population will have to be dramatically reduced as headage payments are phased out. As a result of the current crisis in farming, many farmers are threatening to leave the land, and those that remain may well have to adjust to support mechanisms devoted to environmental protection rather than food production. In 1999 livestock prices were hit by the BSE crisis and by a reduced demand for mutton and beef; on several occasions prices were so low that farmers "dumped" their animals or refused to take them to market. The photograph shows an ewe and her twin lambs on a north Pembrokeshire smallholding. *Further reading: 5,56,65*

83 Cilgwyn, near Newport (078366) The farming crisis

Opposite: With dangerous waters all around the rocky Pembrokeshire coastline and with centuries of intense shipping use in St George's Channel, lights and beacons have been used to assist mariners for over 500 years. One of the most famous -- and profitable -- of all British lighthouses was built by Henry Whitesides on the Smalls in 1776, and during the next hundred years others were built on the South Bishop Rock, Strumble Head, St Ann's Head, Skokholm and Caldey. A lightship was also stationed off St Govan's Head. Under the control of Trinity House they were manned, maintained and improved over the years. Now all of the land-based lighthouses are automatic, and romantic tales of stranded lighthouse keepers, intrepid deliveries of Christmas hampers and so forth have drifted into the history and mythology of the Pembrokeshire coast. The photograph shows the Strumble Head lighthouse, which is vitally important for shipping within Cardigan Bay. *Further reading: 8,13,26,53*

**84 Strumble Head (892413)
The local lighthouses**

**85 Cottages at Newport (058393)
Civic pride and local planning**

Many of the older dwellings of the towns of Pembrokeshire have been demolished to make way for commercial development. For example, the centre of Haverfordwest has been transformed within the last twenty years; many splendid town houses and cottages have been lost, and instead the town has acquired its share of monstrous and unbeautiful supermarkets. However, where urban renewal is making less of an impact, as in the north county towns of St. David's, Fishguard and Newport, there is a justifiable pride in the preservation and renovation of simple homes. It has to be said that the growth of the self-catering holiday market has encouraged property owners in both urban and rural situations to rescue old buildings and refurbish them, keeping many vernacular features in the process. Architects, builders and planners have also had positive roles to play in this respect. Newport is designated by the NPA as a potential "conservation area", but the community is not inclined to cooperate. But has its fair share of civic pride, as these well kept Long Street cottages indicate. There is no pavement, and the exuberant flower border is spilling out over the road.
Further reading: 33,45,64

Prior to 1906 the small fishing ports of Fishguard and Goodwick were sleepy and largely inactive. Then transformation came with the arrival of the railway and the building of a new harbour and rail terminus beneath the cliffs north of Goodwick. The harbour, protected by a long breakwater, was opened with the initiation of a steamer service to Rosslare. Fishguard then attempted to attract ocean-going traffic, even though the harbour was too shallow for the big Cunard liners like the "Mauritania" to tie up at the quayside. In the intense rivalry between the shipping lines before the First World War the use of Fishguard as a terminus could save 40 miles on the New York - Liverpool route; so Cunard Lines used Fishguard from six to eight times a month between 1910 and 1914. The port was also used by the Booth Line and the Blue Funnel Line.

86 Fishguard Harbour (955390)
The Irish ferry service

Nevertheless, Fishguard was never a serious rival to Liverpool and its transatlantic passenger services were not revived after the War. Since the Last War Fishguard has been best known for its sea links with Ireland. The Waterford and Cork passenger services were discontinued in the 1960's, but the ferry operation continues with several sailings each day to Rosslare. The port is now operated by Stena Line, with both a conventional ro-ro vessel and a high-speed Lynx based at the port. The photograph shows the "Koningen Beatrix" leaving the harbour, with Dinas Head in the background. *Further reading: 5,26,36,53*

Many local craft industries, including the woollen industry, declined sadly in the post-war years. No longer do the members of isolated rural communities make their own implements, and domestic articles of pottery, wood, stone and metalwork are now almost always of the mass-produced varieties. Nevertheless, there are a few Pembrokeshire craftsmen who maintain the old skills. In the Welshry traditional woodworking is still practised. Craftsmen produce spoons and ladles, hand-turned spinning-wheels, bowls, cradles, chairs and other furniture. As tourism provides a ready market for local hand-made articles many craft workshops, craft markets and galleries are open to the public. Local artists and sculptors are also active, and summer exhibitions of their work are popular in the main towns. It is perhaps inevitable that a county with such a varied environment and such a high "quality of life" should have provided inspiration for many famous artists, among them Augustus John, Ceri Richards and John Piper. The photograph shows Inger John, who established her candle business in the hamlet of Cilgwyn almost 25 years ago.
Further reading: 5,56,66

87 Cilgwyn Candles (076366)
Local crafts today

Opposite: Pembrokeshire has had a chequered recent history. It can lay claim to the title of "Wales' premier county", having been in existence for 870 years, far longer than any other county in the Principality. In 1974 it was rudely reorganized by the government of the day, and in spite of vociferous and well-organized local protests and massive petitions it was lumped together with Carmarthenshire and Cardiganshire into the conglomerate county of Dyfed. Pembrokeshire people never came to terms with the new enlarged local government arrangement, and fought constantly for the return of their beloved old county. Their battle was won in 1995, and in 1996 the county of Pembrokeshire formally came back into being. There are two main symbols of Pembrokeshire pride, both based in the old county town of Haverfordwest. One is the very successful Pembrokeshire College, and the other (shown in this photo) is the new County Hall on the banks of the Western Cleddau river.
Further reading: 5,43,66,68

88 County Hall, Haverfordwest (954157)
The return of the old County

**89 US Naval "Facility", Brawdy (842237)
The Peace Dividend**

The Second World War resulted in the establishment of hundreds of military sites in Pembrokeshire, including no less than twelve airfields. Most of these sites were wound down with the advent of peace. Nevertheless, during the Cold War some key military installations remained open, including RAF Brawdy, the army camps at Manorbier and Penally, the Castlemartin tank range, and the mine depots at Newton Noyes (Milford) and Trecwn. These were all of great importance to the local economy, providing good-quality military and civilian jobs (for example in engineering and electronics) and bringing large numbers of military families to housing estates in Haverfordwest. With the ending of the Cold War Trecwn and Newton Noyes have closed and have been sold off, with considerable job losses. The old mine depot at Trecwn, incorporating a very beautiful valley with 58 massive tunnels driven into its flanks, was sold to a company called Omega Pacific. An initial friendly welcome from the people of Pembrokeshire turned into outright hostility in 1998 when the company suddenly produced an ill-considered proposal to use the tunnels for nuclear waste storage. Another aspect of the "peace dividend" was seen at Brawdy, where a sinister set of buildings that housed a US naval "facility" was closed and put onto the market. It was common knowledge that the site (shown in the photograph) was a top-secret listening base used for tracking the movements of Soviet submarines in the western approaches; now the strange windowless buildings house a small privately-owned business park. *Further reading: 5,50,53*

In the decades after the Second World war the old market town of Narberth was a sad and somewhat seedy place, too big to be written off and too small to provide a full range of services for the surrounding countryside. However, there has recently been something of a resurgence in the town. Town centre buildings have been refurbished and given new facades and fresh paint; social facilities have been greatly improved; new small business units have been built and occupied by successful businesses; new housing estates have sprung up; and there are new and sophisticated shops. The transformation has taken place partly because of the gutsy determination of local people and partly because a local economic development organisation called SPARC (the South Pembrokeshire Partnership for Action with Rural Communities) has acted as a catalyst. The

90 Narberth town centre (109147)
Urban regeneration

organisation is a locally based, democratically run, grass roots initiative which has no formal links with the local authority. Over the years it has attracted millions of pounds of inward investment to Narberth and the surrounding countryside, much of it from the EU. It has been highly successful in marketing the east-central part of Pembrokeshire (referred to as "The Landsker Borderlands") as a holiday destination. The photograph shows the old Town Hall, parked bravely in the middle of the main shopping street.

Further reading: 5,16,45,58

91 Riverside Development, Haverfordwest (954160)
Town centres versus retail parks

One of the greatest controversies raging in Pembrokeshire at the beginning of the new Millennium relates to the changing pattern of shopping and the role of town centre retail developments. In Haverfordwest the old commercial core of the town, based upon Market Street, High Street and Bridge Street, has declined as a result of a new riverside development built speculatively by private developers, and incorporating retail sales units priced well beyond the reach of old-established family businesses. As has happened elsewhere in the UK, the local authority gave consent for the development having been seduced by grandiose plans and by the obsession with capital investment. The development (seen in the photograph) is indubitably attractive, but some of the retail units have now stood empty for almost a decade. The seepage of commercial activity downhill from the old town has continued with the development of a further retail park on the Bridge Meadow site and with further retail outlets built by national retail companies adjacent to Withybush Hospital. In all cases the motivation has been the desire to cater for the car-based shopper -- which is fine if you happen to own a car and if you don't worry too much about running costs and environmental pollution.......

Further reading: 5, 56,68

As farmers try to come to terms with the current crisis, and as members of the public show growing concerns about pollution, BSE, genetically modified crops and food additives, changes in the rural economy are inevitable. Pembrokeshire is seen as one of the key areas in the UK for the development of organic food production, and many farms have already converted to the exacting Soil Association standards. Farmers' Markets and Farm Shops will become common as farmers seek to reduce the control of the big supermarket chains over the food supply system. The term "sustainable development" is now used with wild abandon by planners and by the rest of us, but what does it actually mean in the countryside? At Brithdir Mawr, near Newport, residents have challenged the National Park planning system by building -- without planning consents -- a number of "low impact" dwellings and other structures, using renewable energy and spring water, and using their land for

92 New cottage, Brithdir Mawr, near Newport (075374) Living lightly on the land

various "non-agricultural" purposes. They argue that they are putting their ideas on sustainable living into practice. However, the NPA has chosen to take enforcement action against the residents, and "the lost tribe of Cilgwyn" has had to cope with massive media coverage. The National Park planners have been inundated with hundreds of furious protests against their supposedly heavy-handed actions; and whatever the outcome of the inevitable public inquiry may be, the issue of sustainable development is now firmly on the planning agenda. The photograph shows a "biodegradable" low-energy house at Brithdir Mawr.
Further reading: 5,6,48,53,67

Nobody knows how many ships -- and seafarers' lives -- have been lost around the Pembrokeshire coast, but there are thousands of recorded shipwrecks. At least 500 wreck locations are known to maritime historians, and the folklore of the county is full of tales of heroic rescue operations by land-based teams and by the crews of the Pembrokeshire lifeboats. For example, in 1877 the St David's lifeboat "Augusta" , which was then based at Porthlysgi, made a famous rescue of nine sailors from the wreck of the "Mystic Tie". In 1920 seven seamen were rescued from the sinking "Hermina" near Needle Rock in Fishguard Bay. One of the most famous rescues was that involving the steamship "Molesey" which went aground on Skomer Island during a fearsome storm in 1929. On that occasion 28 people were rescued by the Angle lifeboat, and seven were lost. During the nineteenth century lifeboats were operating from Tenby, Angle, St David's and Fishguard, and these are still the stations which

93 St Justinian's, near St David's (724251) The lifeboat service

provide assistance in Pembrokeshire's stormiest waters. There have been other short-lived stations at Newport, Little Haven and Solva. Before 1909 all the lifeboats were powered by oars and sails, and they often had to be launched in heavy surf from cumbersome horsedrawn waggons. The modern deepwater vessels are very powerful and are built to sophisticated self-righting designs. In recent years there have been a number of additions to the rescue service in the form of inshore rescue boats with inflatable hulls and powerful outboard motors. The men who volunteer their time to the lifeboat service are skilful and brave, and the local crews are held in high esteem by Pembrokeshire people. The photograph shows the slipway of the lifeboat station at St Justinian's on Ramsey Sound.
Further reading: 7,13,19,26

In the last decade of the Twentieth Century tourism has become the county's major industry in terms of manpower and earnings. Although some local people still look on it as a "Mickey Mouse" industry, many of the companies and individuals who cater for the needs of holidaymakers run sophisticated and high-tech businesses. They invest heavily in new buildings and facilities, use sophisticated marketing techniques, and employ large numbers of people. It is estimated that about 20,000 people in the county are now dependent upon tourism for their income. Some of the most interesting and capital-intensive developments have occurred in South Pembrokeshire's "leisure park belt", outside the National Park where planning constraints are not so tight. Within a few

miles of each other we can now visit Heron's Brook near Narberth, Folly Farm near Begelly, Oakwood near Canaston Bridge, Heatherton Country Sports Park near Tenby, Manor House near St Florence, and the Dinosaur Experience near Gumfreston. There are

many other innovative all-weather holiday centres in other parts of the county, and it can no longer be claimed that Pembrokeshire is a "wet holiday nightmare." The photograph shows visitors (and waterfowl) at Heron's Brook. *Further reading: 5,56,58*

94 Heron's Brook Leisure Park (105138)
The leisure park boom

95 Welsh Wildlife Centre, Cilgerran (187450)
Conserving the future

There is a significant trend in Pembrokeshire today towards what may be called "green tourism". This is a style of tourism which is sustainable in the long term, which depends upon relatively limited capital assets, and which makes virtues of low energy use and low environmental impact. The Wildlife Trust in West Wales has been leading the way in this field for many years, with carefully managed birdwatching holiday visits to Skomer and Skokholm Islands and with sensitive use of its network of nature reserves. The National Park the Countryside Council for Wales, the National Trust and the RSPB also actively promote "low-key" use of sensitive sites, encouraging visitors to walk rather than drive, to observe but not disturb wildlife, and to quietly enjoy the scenery of the coastline. Walking and cycling holidays are growing in popularity each year. Boat trips around the Pembrokeshire islands are also popular, even though skippers are sometimes criticised for approaching bird nesting colonies too closely or for disturbing seals on their breeding beaches. Activities such as cliff climbing and "coasteering" are more controversial, and involve a great deal of self-discipline on the part of operators and participants if wildlife is not to be damaged. The photo shows the Welsh Wildlife Centre near Cilgerran, a key educational resource on environmental matters run by the Wildlife Trust.
Further reading: 5,6,26,53,66

In the Preseli uplands the climate is harsh and the soils are acid and often waterlogged. The natural vegetation is heather moorland with some areas of fell or mountain grassland. Understandably, it has always been difficult to make a good living from agriculture in the highest parishes, and since the Last War many small farms have been abandoned. At the present day sheep rearing is the main occupation in the uplands, although cattle may be kept on the lower slopes. Until quite recently there used to be crops of grass, oats and mixed corn, and potatoes and other root vegetables on the upland fringes. Most of the crops were used as animal feedstuffs. However, with the advent of "specialisation" and EU subsidies many farmers have abandoned cultivation altogether, and now simply cut their best fields for silage. This has made them very vulnerable to political and economic decisions made in London and Brussels. Some of the upland farmers have moved into farm tourism or have diversified in other directions, but they have far fewer options open to them than their colleagues in the lowlands. This photograph shows silage bags in a field near Crymych.

Further reading: 5,52,60,63

96 Farm near Crymych (168332))
A north Pembrokeshire hill farm

Churchyards and other graveyards occupy thousands of acres of Pembrokeshire land.   If we disregard the isolated cromlechs and Bronze Age burial mounds which were used for single and sometimes multiple burials, selected patches of ground have been used as graveyards for 5,000 years at least. For example, at Cerrig y Gof near Newport there is a cluster of five separate Neolithic tombs, and on the slope above the houses of Harbour Village (Goodwick) there is a little cluster of at least four primitive cromlechs. The tribe which built them must have considered the ground on which they stood to be sacred, just as modern graveyards are "consecrated" today. Old graveyards from the time of the Celtic missionaries are known from a number of sites, including St Bride's, where old stone tombs have been eroded by the sea. The graveyards at St

David's, St Dogmaels and on Caldey Island must also be very old, as are the circular churchyards at St Edren's and Maenclochog, both of which are probably pre-Christian.   The majority of the churchyards associated with parish churches have been accumulating bones since the early Middle Ages, and sometimes when space was at a premium old graves had to be re-used. The bones taken out from the most ancient graves

97 Whitchurch Graveyard (799254)
Landscapes of the dear departed

were sometimes stored in Ossuaries like the one in the churchyard at Carew Cheriton. Headstone design and carving is a matter of local tradition; for example, slate slabs were widely used in some areas while limestone or sandstone was used in others. In coastal churchyards there are abundant headstones recording the deaths of merchants and seafarers, some of them dating back to the mid-1700's. Sadly. many of our old graveyards are now in a poor state, overgrown and unloved. The more modern "civic" ones are looked after better, partly because relatives always care for the graves of the recently deceased. Also, the modern trend towards cremation has led to a heavy use of the Parc Gwyn Crematorium near Narberth. The photograph shows the overgrown churchyard at Whitchurch, near Solva. *Further reading: 11,27,40,44*

A considerable acreage of the Pembrokeshire landscape is given over to the pursuit of learning. There have been special buildings used as schools and colleges ever since the Middle Ages, and St Mary's College adjacent to the cathedral in St David's must be one of the oldest. Some of the vestries and halls associated with the nonconformist chapels were used in the late 1700's as venues for the famous "circulating schools". Later on, in Victorian times, there was a move towards universal education, and hundreds of council schools were built all over Pembrokeshire. Some of them are still in use today, although most have long since been replaced with light, airy and pleasant new buildings where study becomes a pleasure rather than a penance. Playgrounds and playing fields (and

98 Pembrokeshire College (945145)
Landscapes of learning

recently, school car parks) also feature prominently when you look down on Pembrokeshire from the air. The most notable recent addition to the local educational landscape is the Pembrokeshire College near Merlin's Bridge, which now provides further education for thousands of youngsters and adults on a wide range of courses every year. The photo shows the front entrance of the College.

Further reading: 5,59,68

One of the most fascinating features of modern life is the obsession with instant communications. Telecommunications and information technology have insinuated their way into our lives to an extent undreamt of even a decade ago. For many years we have accepted spindly radio masts held up by wires, and television transmitters and boosters. But now we have satellite signal receiver dishes fixed to the walls of thousands of dwellings, and the mobile phone is menacing all parts of the countryside. Strange pylons and lattice towers are appearing on many of the hilltops of Pembrokeshire; local people are not at all sure who puts them up and what they do. They are almost as mysterious as the strange towers near Templeton which are reputed to have something to do with the MoD. Some of the new towers presumably send useful signals relating to

**99 Mast near Wallaston Cross (925015)
The information revolution**

the work of the emergency services (police, ambulance, coast guard and fire brigade), but most of them are erected by commercial mobile phone operators who are competing with other mobile phone operators. Where will this all lead us? Will the Pembrokeshire landscape be covered eventually with a forest of these things, simply to satisfy our mania for being in contact with the whole of the rest of the world for twenty-four hours a day? Perhaps, at the end of one millennium and the beginning of another, one might be forgiven for yearning, just a little, for the pace of life, and the quiet and gentle priorities, of Pembrokeshire as it was.
Further reading: 5,29,67

Further Reading

SECTION ONE: FEATURES OF THE NATURAL LANDSCAPE

1 Bassett, D.A and Bassett, M.G. **Geological Excursions in South Wales and the Forest of Dean** (Cardiff, 1971)
2 Evans, R.O. and John, B.S. **The Pembrokeshire Landscape** (Tenby, 1973)
3 Ellis-Gruffydd, I.D. **Rocks and Scenery of the Pembrokeshire Coast** (NPA, 1988))
4 John, B.S. **The Rocks: Geology of Pembrokeshire**, Pembrokeshire Handbooks (Abercastle Publications, 1995 reprint)
5 John, B.S. **Pembrokeshire: Past and Present** (Greencroft Books, 1995)
6 Saunders, D. (ed) **The Nature of West Wales** (Barracuda Books, 1986)

SECTION TWO: THE EVOLUTION OF THE MAN-MADE LANDSCAPE

7 Bennett, T. **Welsh Shipwrecks** (Vols. 1, 2, 3) (Haverfordwest, 1981)
8 Brinton, P. and Worsley, R. **Open Secrets** (Gomer, 1987)
9 Carradice, P. **The Last Invasion** (Pontypool, 1992)
10 Charles, B.G. **The Place-Names of Pembrokeshire** (Nat Library of Wales, 2 vols, 1992)
11 Children, G. and Nash, G. **Neolithic Sites of Cardiganshire, Carmarthenshire and Pembrokeshire** (Logaston Press, 1997)
12 Davies, P.B.S. **Dewisland Limekilns** (Merrivale Publications, 1989)
13 Davies, P. B. S. **Deadly Perils** (Merrivale Publications, 1992)
14 Davies, R. **Old Pembrokeshire** (Gomer, 1988)
15 Edwards, G. **The Coal Industry in Pembrokeshire** (FSC, 1963)
16 Fenton, R. **A Historical Tour Through Pembrokeshire** (1810, republished by Dyfed CC, 1994)
17 Fitzgerald, M. **Pembrokeshire Churches** (Rosedale Publications, 1989)
18 Gale, J. **The Maenclochog Railway** (private pub, 1992)
19 Goddard, T. **Pembrokeshire Shipwrecks** (Llandybie, 1983)
20 Howells, B. (ed) **Pembrokeshire County History, Vol 3** (Haverfordwest, 1987)
21 Howells, R. **Across the Sounds to the Pembrokeshire Islands** (Gomer, 1972)
22 Howells, R. **Tenby Old and New** (Gomer, 1981)
23 Howells, R. **Old Saundersfoot** (Gomer, 1977)
24 James, D.W. **St David's and Dewisland** (Cardiff, 1981)
25 James, D.W. **Twice to St David's** (Gomer, 1995)
26 John, B.S. **Pembrokeshire**

Coast Path: National Trail Guide (Aurum/HMSO, 1997)

27 John, T. Sacred Stones (Gomer, 1994)

28 Jones, F. Historic Houses of Pembrokeshire (Brawdy Books, 1996)

29 Jones, F. Treasury of Historic Pembrokeshire (Brawdy Books, 1998)

30 McKay, K. The Story of Milford Haven (MH Museum, 1993)

31 McKay, K. A Vision of Greatness (Chevron, 1989)

32 Miles, D. A Book on Nevern (Gomer, 1998)

33 Miles, D. The Ancient Borough of Newport in Pembrokeshire (Dyfed CC, 1995)

34 Miles, D. History of Haverfordwest (Gomer, 1999)

35 Molloy, P. And they blessed Rebecca (Llandysul, 1983)

36 Morris, J. The Railways of Pembrokeshire(Tenby, 1981)

37 Owen, George, The Desc-ription of Pembroke-shire (1603, ed D. Miles, Llandysul, 1994)

38 Price, M.R.C. Industrial Saundersfoot (Gomer, 1982)

39 Rees, N. St David of Dewisland (Gomer, 1992)

40 Rees, S. Dyfed: Cadw Guide to Ancient and Historic Wales (Cadw/HMSO, 1992)

41 Rees, V. South -West Wales (Shell Guide, 1976)

42 Richards, A.J. The Slate Quarries of Pembrokeshire (Carreg Gwalch, 1998)

43 Richards, B. Haverfordwest my Grandstand (Haverfordwest Civic Society, 1994)

44 Salter, M. The Old Parish Churches of South-West Wales (Folly Publications, 1994)

45 Salter, M. The Castles of South-West Wales (Folly Publications, 1996)

46 Scott, V. Inferno 1940 (Western Telegraph, 1980)

47 Sharkey, J. (editor) Ogham Monuments in Wales (Llanerch, 1992)

48 Sime, J. St David's Peninsula (Pebbles Books, 1999)

49 Smith, P. Houses of the Welsh Countryside (Royal Commission on Ancient Monuments, 1988)

50 Thomas, R.J.C. Survey of 19th and 20th Century Military Buildings of Pembroke-shire (NPA, 1994)

51 Timmins, H.T. Nooks and Corners of Pembrokeshire (1895, reprinted 1998)

52 Toulson, S. and Forbes, C. The Drover's Roads of Wales: Pembrokeshire and the South (Whittet Books, 1992)

53 Wright, C.J. A Guide to the Pembrokeshire Coast Path (Constable, 1986)

SECTION THREE: RECENT CHANGES IN THE LANDSCAPE

54 Aitchison, J and Carter, H. A Geography of the Welsh

Language 1961 - 1991 (Cardiff 1994)

55 Carradice, P. **The Book of Pembroke Dock** (Buckingham, 1990)

56 Cowsill, M. **Pembrokeshire in Profile** (Haven Publications, 1991)

57 Davies, P.B.S. **Forgotten Mines** (Merrivale, 1990)

58 Dyfed Archaeological Trust. **The Landsker Borderlands -- history and landscape** (SPARC 1992)

59 Environment Agency Wales, **Cleddau and Pembroke-shire Coast** (LEAP Consultation Report, 1999)

60 Fenna, J. **Heritage Walks in Pembrokeshire** (Sigma, 1997)

61 Fitzgerald, M. **Pembrokeshire Architecture** (Rosedale Publications, 1989)

62 Jermy, R.C. **The Railways of Porthgain and Abereiddi** (Oakwood Press, 1986)

63 John, B.S. **Walking in the Presely Hills** (NPA, 1989)

64 John, B.S. **Beneath the Mountain** (Greencroft Books, 1998)

65 John, B.S. (ed) **Bluestone Country: The Carningli Walks** (Newport Town Council, 1999)

66 Miles, D. (ed.) **Pembrokeshire Coast National Park**, National Park Guide No 10, (HMSO 1973)

67 Pembrokeshire Coast National Park Authority, **National Park Plan** (Haverfordwest, 1996)

68 Richards, B. **Changing Face of Haverfordwest** (Haver-fordwest Civic Society, 1992)

69 Saunders, D., Donovan, J. and Phillips, J. **A Waterway for Wildlife** (Dyfed Wildlife Trust, 1991)

70 Scott, V. **An Experience Shared** (Laleham Publications, 1992)

71 Sharkey, J. **Pilgrim Ways** (Ancient Landscapes, 1994)

72 Sutcliffe, A. **A Tourists Guide to the Pembrokeshire Islands** (private pub, 1990)

Whitesands Bay (Martin John)

Place-name Index